# Battleground Europe

# ARRAS

# Vimy Ridge

# To my Mother and Father

# Battleground Europe

# ARRAS

# Vimy Ridge

## Nigel Cave

**LEO COOPER**
London

First published in 1996
Reprinted 1997

LEO COOPER

an imprint of
Pen & Sword Books Ltd
47 Church Street, Barnsley, South Yorkshire S70 2AS

**ISBN 0 85052 399 0**

A CIP catalogue record of this book is available
from the British Library

Printed by Redwood Books Limited
Trowbridge, Wiltshire

*For up-to-date information on other titles produced under the
Leo Cooper imprint, please telephone or write to:*

Pen & Sword Books Ltd, FREEPOST, 47 Church Street
Barnsley, South Yorkshire S70 2AS
Telephone 01226 734222

*Opposite:* **The road leading from Arras to Mont St Eloi, Winter, 1915.**

# CONTENTS

# ACKNOWLEDGEMENTS

Many people have helped me in putting this book together. My first tribute is to the authors of all the various material which makes up the bulk of this book - the writers of Regimental Divisional and Official histories, the officers who maintained the War Diaries, the staff officers who wrote up reports and the men who have got their war experiences into print.

I am most grateful to Richard Brucciani who took two days off work, flew me in his plane over the battlefields of Loos, Arras and the Somme and managed to perform without complaint all the aerobatic manoeuvres for which I asked in order to get some photograph or the other. Various friends on Battlefields Tours have spent longer than they might have expected on the Ridge and so I am grateful to Paul and David Fisher, Dr Graham Keech and Col Dick Burge for humouring me. On a mad dash to Arras over a weekend in January to finalize the photography I was accompanied by two past pupils from Ratcliffe, Sam Mudd and Barney Petty. Fortunately the ulterior motive (viz, pushing the car out of trouble) did not arise.

Numerous people have helped by giving freely of their own knowledge of Vimy and its area. In particular I would like to single out Lt Col (Retd) Philip Robinson RE who conducted an underground survey for the Canadian Memorial Committee and who has deluged me with information and paper which has proved fascinating. Distance is the chief obstacle from my sitting at the feet of Tom Gudmestad who spends as much time as he can, when he can get away from Seattle, on the northern Arras battlefield and who probably knows more about it than anyone.

Regimental Museums have once more proved to be a source of useful information. My chief debt in this regard is to Lt Col Pat Love, Worcesters, who has a deep respect for the achievements of his Regiment in the Great War and has been a fount of information. I have also received the assistance of the Regimental Museums of the Queen's Lancashire Regt, of the Argyll and Sutherland Highlanders and of the Queen's Own Highlanders. I am also grateful to them for the loan of documents and photographs.

Once more I am obliged to the Commonwealth War Graves Commission for their assistance, most notably in the matter of the loan of registers. Any visit to the battlefields has to include time spent in cemeteries. Many of the cemeteries in the area of the Ridge are more than usually isolated - Petit Vimy, Zouave Valley and Givenchy-en-Gohelle to mention a few. All the more impressive then to find these returfed and Villers Station undergoing the same treatment; even lonely and neglected (by the visitors) Thelus Cemetery was having new turf laid. Visitors come and visitors go, but the CWGC is standing firm on the promises made in its charter.

I am thankful to the following for allowing me to publish extracts, photographs or maps: Tom Gudmestad, The Worcestershire Regimental Musem, Col Philip Robinson, Dr MS Rosenbaum, Sono Nis Press (The Journal of Private Fraser), Lancelot Press (Gunner Ferguson's Diary), the Crown Copyright Service, the Peter Taylor Photographic Library, author Mike Stedman, the Commonwealth War Graves Commission and the Museums of La Targette and Notre Dame de Lorette.

I am indebted to those who have looked through earlier drafts of this book and have made suggestions and corrections. Both George Friendship and Paul Fisher have better things to do with their time, but manfully waded through the script. My father, Col Terry Cave CBE, did the same, came up with various source suggestions, let me lose on his Great War book collection, and of course came on tour with me. We have been doing these annually (more or less) since 1980. My mother never comes on a battlefield tour, and never complains when another week in France and Flanders looms and she is left to guard the house. I dedicate this book to them both.

# INTRODUCTION

How many people come to Vimy Ridge, visit the Canadian Memorial Park and leave an hour or so later having admired the memorial, wandered over the preserved trenches and possibly gone underground in the Grange Subway? What impression do they have when they go? Perhaps they think that this was a battle fought in isolation for a notable landmark, which chiefly involved the Canadians and which was one of the great decisive battles of the war. They might be justified in thinking so.

The capture of Vimy Ridge in April 1917 was an important event and was a considerable victory. One might question whether the heroic Canadian defence at St Julien against the first use of poison gas on the Western Front in the battle of Second Ypres might have a greater claim or the outstanding contribution of the Canadian Forces in the Hundred Days of 1918 which led to Germany's defeat. Vimy Ridge was important because it saw the birth of a Canadian Army, and with it the greater realisation of national consciousness. That alone justifies the memorial; but the battle was a fine feat of arms in its own right.

Lost in this understandable concentration on the Canadians is the contribution of the armies that stood in this sector prior to the arrival of the Canadian Corps in October 1916. There is very little left to indicate their achievement. The French army made great sacrifices in 1915 and the achievement of some of her divisions - most notably the Moroccan - stands with the greatest of wartime exploits. A visit to the Notre Dame de Lorette Cemetery overpoweringly shows the sacrifice that was made. A tour of the ground over which the battles of 1915 were fought will show just how difficult was the task that faced the French. In the spring of 1916 the French armies departed from the Arras region never to return during the Great War. In their place came British troops from an army which was expanding at a phenomenal rate. Whilst great things were planned on the Somme and were then carried out the troops here clung on to the unsatisfactory positions on Vimy Ridge whilst specialist Tunnelling Companies worked feverishly underground to overcome the German mining threat.

Finally the Canadians arrived in the autumn of 1916, relieved from their hard fought battles around Courcelette and Regina Trench on the Somme. They played their role in the 1917 Battle of Arras, the British contribution to the grandiose schemes of General Nivelle.

The region around Arras has seen many battles, and the dominant high ground of Vimy Ridge has played an important part in many of them. The Emperor Valentinian spent time here during his Gallic campaigns and the village of Etrun still shows signs of his fortifications. Men at arms involved in the Hundred Years' War fought nearby; Charles V and his successors Philip II and Philip IV had armies battling nearby for European supremacy with their French counterparts. Vimy Ridge played a vital part in Marlborough's campaign of 1711 - there is much more to the military history of Arleux and Monchy le Preux than their place in the battles of 1917. Some of the decisive fighting in the saving of the British Army in 1940 took place around Arras, when Frankforce struggled to hold up the encircling German Army. North European war does not seem to be able to avoid Arras.

This book is a guide to aspects of the war around Vimy Ridge, most particularly as it affected the British Army. The biggest gap from the work is the contribution of the Germans to events. The book makes no claim to be all-encompassing, but aims to give the visitor a reasonably balanced tour of the battlefield and  of the events, units and personalities that were  involved in the war and of the memorials, cemeteries, museums and remains of battle that mark their work.

The best way to use the book is to read the whole thing through and familiarise yourself with place names, events and the maps. Having done that, the tours are designed to take you over the whole of the area covered by the book, and each one, where appropriate, refers the tourer to the relevant chapters in the book. There is a section on further reading and advice on what the visitors should have with them. Much of the damage done to nature by shellfire and mine blast is disappearing; but with a little imagination and a willingness to learn it is possible to understand so much more by a visit to this battlefield than simply reading about it in books.

**Deserted trenches at Souchez, north of Arras.**

# ADVICE TO TRAVELLERS

Vimy Ridge is easily accessible from the Calais - Paris autoroute; take the Vimy/Arras Central exit and this comes out on the Arras - Lens road. There are considerable road works going on at the time of writing (January 1996) and this was one of the major reasons why the book was confined in scope to the crest of Vimy Ridge - the extent and consequences of this road programme on battlefield memorials and their access is not clear at the moment.

The approach to Arras is slightly hair-raising on a first acquaintance so I would recommend arriving outside of rush hour times should you wish to go into the city. This is the obvious place to stay, and I would recommend the Hotel Univers, though after a recent refurbishment the prices have gone up. It is in the centre of Arras (as is the Ibis Hotel) and this gives plenty of options for shopping and eating as well as the pleasure of being able to stroll of an evening through the Grande Place and the Place des Heros. There is an underground car park under the Grande Place, and the Univers has limited car parking in its courtyard. By following the signs to Cambrai through Arras (not on the motorway!) the driver will find signs for Hotel Formule 1, a convenience chain of hotels. This one is on the outskirts. The hotels are simple, clean and offer a room that sleeps a maximum of three for a flat rate price of about £20, breakfast being extra.

Should the visitor be a caravaner or a camper, then follow the road on towards Cambrai and, just beyond Monchy le Preux, will be found a turning to the left to Boiry Notre Dame. The campsite is also indicated. It is at the eastern end of the village and I can recommend the place, having used it for the last fifteen years. There is a bar, showers, UK style lavatories and various games - tennis, mini golf etc to while away the time. It is about a fifteen to twenty minutes drive from the centre of Arras.

I would recommend that the visitor brings a cool bag to hold the necessary ingredients for a picnic lunch, along with a sharp knife for the baguettes and a corkscrew/bottle-opener for the liquid refreshment. Stout footwear is essential and walking boots are preferable, especially if the weather has been poor for a while. A plastic bag to put the muddy boots in on returning to the car is equally vital. A compass is useful for getting bearings. Binoculars are always handy. A camera with a zoom lens, no matter how limited, is recommended. A tripod might be useful if it is anticipated that you will want to take photographs of headstones or names on memorials. Purchase your film in the UK - it is much cheaper there. Good maps are most important. The Institut

Geographique National produce a number of different scale maps - I would recommend the 1:100000 for navigation (Green Series 2 and 4); the 1:50000 for more detailed work (2406 Arras, Orange Series - uses shading to show topographical details) and the Rolls Royce of them all, the 1:25000 (Blue Series 2406 Est Arras). Also most useful is the Michelin overprinted map available from the CWGC (address below). This is Map No 53 and has marked on it very nearly all the Commonwealth War Graves and Cemeteries.

You should have a First Aid Box and some paracetamol to help ward off the effects of overindulgence with native produce from the night before. Ensure that your tetanus booster is up to date just in case you should be scratched by old barbed wire or some other rusty metal object connected to the war or not. A notebook, pencils and pens are necessary if you want to remember what the photographs are when you get them back from the developers. Otherwise you can be left scratching your head wondering why on earth you took a picture of a pleasant enough French field. As a tip, when you take pictures of the remains of craters, trenches or whatever it is always a good idea to have someone or something in the picture as well so that an idea of scale is achieved and (especially in the case of trenches) an idea of depth. Please also take the time to sign in at the cemetery registers - these are used by the War Graves for statistical purposes, and it is essential that we give that organisation as much support as we can in these days of financial stringency (has there ever been a time when there wasn't financial stringency?). Get a form E1 11 for reciprocal medical cover (obtainable from a Post Office) but always take proper insurance, vehicle and personal. Do not even think about bringing a metal detector. The warning signs at Vimy Ridge are not there for decoration - the

The old battlefields can still present a danger to the unwary in the form of rusting ordnance. Here a collection of various size calibre shells await collection by a bomb disposal squad and the destruction by means of a controlled explosion.

ground still has plenty of deadly relics in the form of shells (explosive and gas) and grenades and they are all still potentially lethal. Use sensible precautions and leave such things alone. The authorities at the Vimy Memorial are very sensitive about maintaining the dignity of the place. Therefore, no picnicking anywhere within its boundaries, keep to the paths and no transistor radios. There is no reason why one should not picnic in other British cemeteries in the area - they are, after all, meant to recreate the atmosphere of an English garden. This should be done, needless to say, with simple propriety and just ensure that you leave the place as spotless as when you first found it.

Visiting a battlefield is a rewarding experience which has much to tell us about the past, about the cost of war and about the tenacity and bravery of men. I very much hope that this guide helps to achieve those purposes.

Enquiries about overprinted Michelin maps and about the location of graves should be made to:

Enquiries,
Commonwealth War Graves Commission,
2 Marlow Road, Maidenhead,
BERKS SL6 7DX

As preparation for a visit to the Great War battlefields I would strongly recommend a visit, if practicable, to the National Army Museum near the Royal Hospital, Chelsea and to the Imperial War Museum in Lambeth. The museum shop is likely to have one or two of the titles in the recommended reading.

From the early formation of the cemeteries great
care was taken clearly to mark every grave and to
identify the remains.

# MAPS

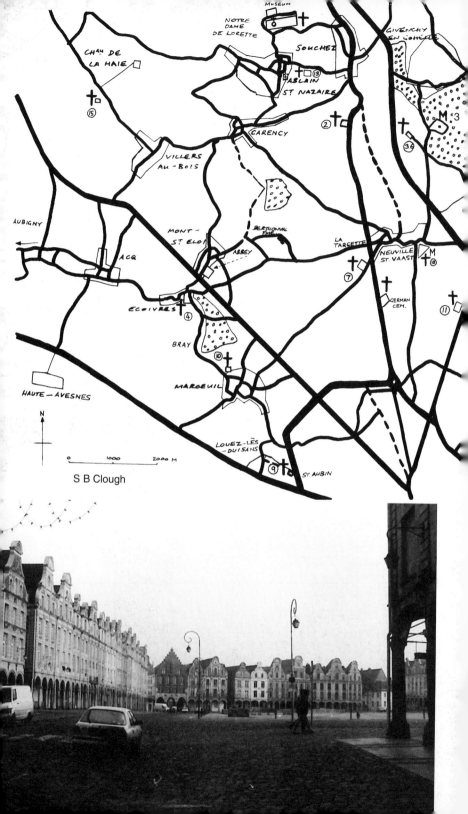

MUSEUM

NOTRE
DAME
DE LORETTE

GIVENCHY
EN GOHELLE

SOUCHEZ

CH<sup>AU</sup> DE
LA HAIE

ABLAIN
ST NAZAIRE

⑬

✝
⑮

② ✝

✝
③⑥

M 3

CARENCY

VILLERS
AU - BOIS

AUBIGNY

BERTHONVAL
FM<sup>E</sup>

MONT -
ST ELOI

ABBEY

LA TARGETTE

ACQ

NEUVILLE
ST. VAAST

✝ M
⑩

✝
⑦

ECOIVRES ✝
④

✝
GERMAN
CEM.

✝
⑪

BRAY

✝
⑩

MAROEUIL

N

HAUTE - AVESNES

0        1000        2000 M

S B Clough

LOUEZ - LÈS
- DUISANS

⑨ ✝
ST. AUBIN

Map left: The area today. See Cemeteries' (†) and Memorials' (M) sections for Key.

Map right: The area in 1915.

Bottom left: Grande Place, Arras on a Sunday morning, January 1996.

Below: The same scene in 1917.

## Chapter One

## 1915: THE YEAR OF THE FRENCH EFFORT

**See map page 14**
The English speaking visitor to this part of the battlefields is naturally drawn to the Canadian Memorial Park situated on Vimy Ridge. Consequently, the enormous efforts of the French Tenth Army in the fighting on either side of the Bethune - Arras road in 1915 is all too frequently ignored. This chapter tries, somewhat inadequately, to redress the balance a little and describes some of the heaviest fighting that took place, most particularly in May 1915.

By the late autumn of 1914 it had become clear that the Western Front had become more or less stabilised. The French army had suffered enormous losses. Between a quarter and a third of their total casualties in the whole of the war were lost in these early months. However as winter drew in, the Germans had begun to withdraw some troops from the west to face a resurgent Russian army in the east and Joffre, the French Commander in Chief, was eager to take whatever benefit might be extracted from this situation. The Tenth Army, holding the Artois Front around Arras was considered capable of launching such an attack, which it did in December and early January.

1915 was to be the year in which Artois and the Champagne dominated as areas of France's offensive action against the invader. The Arras area had much to offer as a launch pad to push the Germans from the sacred soil of France. Vimy Ridge dominated the ground to the east, and the series of German railheads and the lateral railway system that enabled reinforcements to be transferred along the front would be enticingly close. The ground offered the possibility of reasonable freedom of movement, and the possibility of using some of France's cavalry divisions. The British armies were close by and could be

brought in on a joint offensive; the French would be delighted to see her allies carrying rather more of the burden of war.

There were two major offensives known as the Second Battle of Artois, from May 9th continuing until June 18th, and the Third Battle of Artois, from September 25th coming to an end on October 11th. The British actions in support of these were the Battles of Aubers Ridge and Festubert in May and Loos in September. In horrendous fighting on the French front, from just north of the Lorette spur to east of Arras, the French suffered some 150,000 casualties. This figure does not include those victims who died in some quite heavy attacks that were aimed at clearing the Lorette heights in the early months of the year.

In these attacks were some great moments; perhaps most notably the capture of Hill 140 on the crest of the Ridge by the Moroccan Division. This they achieved after an advance of four thousand or so yards within two hours of leaving their assault trenches at 10.00 am on May 9th. The problem of limited reserves and the need to hold them far back in the rear to cover the whole of the front under attack meant that these could not arrive before German counter-attacks had removed the stubborn and courageous soldiers of this regular division.

Much of the action of these battles took place in the area covered by this guide and the ground fought over and gained is indicated on the accompanying map to this chapter. The battles provided important lessons for the combatants. It became apparent that a breakthrough against prepared and well fortified positions was possible and that far more artillery of heavy calibre was required. The munitions production of the allies was sadly inadequate and the Germans were masters in the skills of trench warfare. At the end of the day, and despite some gains, notably the commanding heights of Lorette, the battles had achieved nothing of strategic importance (not even relief for their hard pressed Russian allies). Indeed the new line which was occupied provided real difficulties for the allied defenders, as the British were to discover when they took over the sector in March 1916. Much of it was under direct German observation including the communications system to the rear areas. Events elsewhere were to ensure that this sector became relatively quiet that year, though such a description might not have been the one that would spring to the lips of its defenders!

**The route** for this sector should take the better part of a morning, starting at the huge German cemetery to the south of La Targette. This is a quite stunning revelation of the cost of the war - crosses by the thousand as far as the eye can see and most with four names on their arms. It is suitable that the cemetery should be sited here, for it lies on a part of the old front line known as the *Maison Blanche* sector from

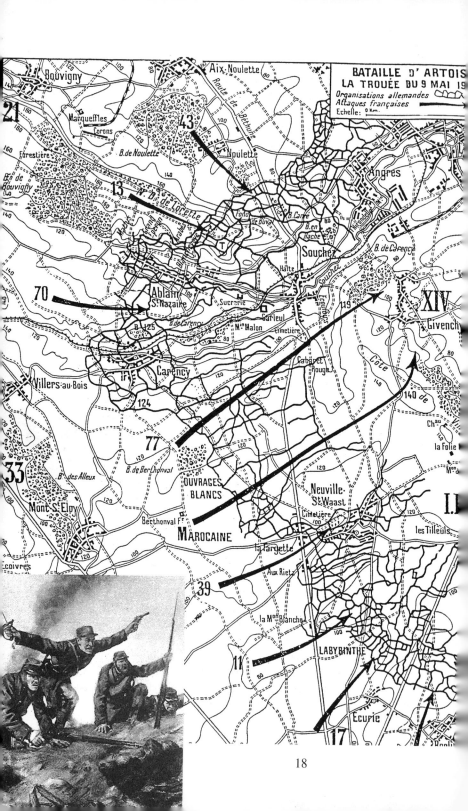

the house that stands on the west side of the D937. A few hundred yards to the south east lay a sector known as the Labyrinth, where thousands of soldiers died in the fighting of 1915.

This great complex of trenches was almost a complete unknown to the French, at least from the ground. Aerial photography (and the French had made exhaustive use of this new contribution to warfare in the preparation for the battle) had revealed an extraordinarily complex system that appeared impregnable. A newspaper correspondent of the time described it as follows:

'Possibly never has a similar stronghold been planned and constructed..... Inside it there is a complete and cunning maze, containing every species of death dealing device known to science, including numbers of gas and inflammable liquid engines. Underground tunnels, coupled with mines, compete with small fortresses containing guns for the better destruction of the daring invaders. In a maze one constantly turns corners to meet blank walls of hedge. In the Labyrinth such corners are death traps, and from their subterranean refuge bodies of the enemy are liable to appear to the rear of the advancing attackers. The Labyrinth is linked up by underground tunnels to Neuville St Vaast, and probably to Thelus, near Vimy. Anyhow, it is an integral and consummately important part of this fortress land - an entire district which constitutes one concentrated fortress.'

On May 9th the 11th Division attacked over the ground which forms part of the cemetery, aiming to take the German positions to the right of Neuville St Vaast. Its right flank came under fire from the Labyrinth; and only the most tenuous toehold was made in this great complex by the 39th Division. The fighting for the Labyrinth lasted well over a month, the French finally claiming it on June 17th. A French officer described the fighting as follows:

'The passages in which we were advancing were 18 ft. deep, and often 24 ft. or more. The water was sweating through in all directions and the sickly smell was intolerable. Imagine, too, that for three weeks we were not able to get rid of the dead bodies, amongst which we used to live night and day! One burrow, 120 ft. long, took us thirteen days of ceaseless fighting to conquer entirely. The Germans had placed barricades, trapdoors and traps of all descriptions. When we stumbled we risked being impaled on bayonets treacherously hidden in holes lightly covered with earth. And all this went on in almost complete darkness. We had to use pocket electric lamps and advance with the utmost caution.'

**Time to read a newspaper and have a smoke in a captured German trench after the successful French attack at Neuville St Vaast in May, 1915.**

Perhaps a certain amount of literary license has been employed, but there is no doubting the ferocity of what took place on and under this now peaceful pastureland. The last vestiges of the fighting that took place in these fields, a few remaining mine craters, have now been filled in. The huge German cemetery graphically illustrates the ferocity of the conflict.

**The driver** has two options for the next destination, Neuville St Vaast. Turn left, and immediately at the southern end of the cemetery turn left again along a farm road which runs into Neuville. When driving alongside the cemetery look to the right as it was in these fields that the Labyrinth was situated. You may wish to stop along the road and look behind you to get some idea of the view the Germans would have had of the advancing French. Alternatively the driver should turn right along the D937 and head for Neuville St Vaast.

The cemetery of Neuville St Vaast is still in its original position at the eastern extremity of the village. It became a bitterly divided battleground, with trenches running through it. A Canadian gunner described the digging of a gunpit there in March 1917:

'In one corner was an emergent head with long flaxen tresses, and from the walls pairs of feet and thigh-bones protruded. The ghoulish surroundings heightened the boys' sense of humour. On arrival for successive stages of the job they stroked the flaxen tresses and hung their tin lids on pulled out thigh-bones.'

On May 9th the 39th Division had made excellent progress, avoiding the German defensive barrage as it crossed No Man's Land and swept through the hamlets of Aux Rietz (often spelt Au Ritz or Au Riez) and la Targette. The German resistance stiffened, and the cemetery was captured and lost a couple of times before the French established themselves on its western side. Primitive barricades were erected across the streets of the village. This rather sleepy place dominated the communiques of the first few days of the battle; the Germans had transformed each house into a fort by use of cement and a network of tunnels that eventually required the systematic destruction of each house by artillery. It was not until June 9th that the village finally fell; and by that time it had been utterly destroyed.

**Returning** towards the D937, on your right just before the crossroads you will see a strange war memorial. A hand, grasping a flame, arises from the debris of a (representational) destroyed bunker. The bracelet that adorns the wrist represents a French identity disc. I would strongly urge the visitor to proceed across the D937 and visit the museum opposite. A ticket for this museum and that at Notre Dame de Lorette may be purchased and it is substantially cheaper than paying for two separate entries. Near these crossroads were entrances to the subterranean works of the *Ouvrages Blancs* and *Maison Blanche*

**A communication trench dug by the Germans through a street in Neuville St Vaast - now in the hands of the French.**

Commander-in-Chief of the French Armies, General Joffre, commiserates with one of his wounded men.

sectors of the line. On May 9th the land on which the museum stands was just on the German Front Line.

**Return** to the D937 heading north, and take the next minor road on the left to Carency. This road runs along, or just behind, the German front line of May 9th. After a kilometre or so, to the left, some twelve hundred yards distance, is Berthonval Farm and, soon afterwards and much closer to the road, is Berthonval Wood (on modern maps called *Bois l'Abbe*). It was from this area that the Morrocan Division, forming part of Petain's XXXIII Corps, launched its strikingly successful attack that took it on to the crest of Vimy Ridge.

The attack cost it heavily, losing three battalion commanders killed out of the four Foreign Legion battalions that formed part of the Division. The Memorial to the Moroccans on Hill 140 (Hill 145 to the British) pays tribute to these battalions, and in particular to the Czech, Greek and Polish companies that formed a part of them. The Czech cemetery and memorial to the Poles and Czechs will be pointed out later in this itinerary. The ground to the west of the road had been captured by the French during fighting in December 1914 and January 1915. This fighting was carried out in appalling weather conditions and resulted in a quagmire of clinging mud that weighed down uniforms, made movement extremely difficult and served to jam rifles. French soldiers in the area became known as 'the mud men of Artois'.

Carency was a tremendously strong position garrisoned by the Germans with four battalions of infantry and a large presence of engineers. After the fighting

French machine gun team operating from hastily dug trenches at Neuville St Vaast.

presence of engineers. After the fighting in early 1915, the French began a systematic programme of mine warfare, detonating a large number of mines in an attempt to bring their line closer to that of the Germans. These mines were especially concentrated to the west of the village (there are insignificant traces of only a few of them now); so much so that an attack on the village from this direction was precluded by the devastated nature of the ground. The attack on May 9th was launched from the south with the aim of cutting the Souchez road and consequently the garrison from the main body. Twenty thousand shells were piled into the village; some efforts were also made from the north west and in addition seventeen mines were fired at 6.45 am in this sector.

**Drive through** the village and stop by the Church to spend some time looking at the position held by the Germans. The houses were all fortified and there were numerous subterranean passages the whole being protected by redoubts on the rising ground around the village. When the fighting ceased on May 9th the only communications that the garrison had were to Ablain St Nazaire to the north, and even this route was under considerable threat.

**Proceed north** through the village to the high ground to the north east. There is not much space to stop here, but the visitor will see the remnants of a large quarry to the right of the road, which at the time of writing is being filled in. During the battle this was a principal part of the German defences and the attack on Carency reached its climax both here and on this ridge. Once this position was taken (on May 12th) the garrison surrendered, and over a thousand prisoners were taken.

**Proceeding** a few hundred yards beyond the quarry the ground opens out, and excellent views may be seen. To the south is the crest of the ridge where the assault began, and beyond the ruined towers of Mont St Eloi Abbey; to the east may be seen Carency Wood and Hill 125, whilst to the north lies the looming presence of the Lorette spur.

Lieutenant General Sir Henry Wilson, then serving with the British Military Mission with Joffre, watched the start of the offensive from trenches just forward of Mont St Eloi:

'There, in front, was the whole panorama. All the French and Boche trenches, the wire and communicating trenches with the tremendous roar of the artillery and shells bursting ceaselessly over the Boche lines and way back over their batteries.

The Frenchmen began to fire at 0600 hours and fired till 1000

Above: German soldiers in one of the underground caverns that served as shelter for the invaders. A concert is being held in this one - 'every Wednesday'- according to the original caption.

Above: One of the underground caverns today in the village of La Targette. The present owner has put in roof supports to make it safer for visitors.

Left: Storming a fortified cellar at Carency during the French May 1915 offensive.

hours. No living person has ever before heard or seen such a thing. The shells passing over my head made one steady hiss.'

**Return to Carency** and take the road northwards to Ablain St Nazaire. At a suitable point stop and view Ablain, the route east towards Souchez and the Lorette heights above. Note how the ground falls away from the Lorette heights in a series of north-south spurs, the individual capture of which cost the French heavily. The fighting here lasted all through the first phase of the offensive, and came to a sticky halt in the mud around the sugar refinery, the village and the heights having eventually been captured. To clear the village took three weeks, from May 9th to May 29th. The fighting was particularly fierce in a number of prominent parts of the village; these include the spur of the White Way, to the north west of the ruined church, on May 21st.

**As you enter Ablain** from Carency you will see the cemetery on your right; here heavy fighting took place on May 28th; it was cut off by artillery from reinforcements from the east, and was carried by the point of the bayonet, producing four hundred prisoners. The ruined church and presbytery proved a particularly hard nut to crack; by the time the French launched their final assault on May 29th on the defending three companies they had captured the village to the north, west and south; only twenty of the defenders remained alive to be taken prisoner. A German officer, Captain Sievert, had noted on May 17th:

'When we were in the ravine of Souchez we did not believe that there could be any worse position. Here we perceive that it is possible. Not only are we exposed to frontal and flank fire, but the French are firing at our backs from the slopes of the plateau of Notre Dame de Lorette.'

**Proceed out of Ablain** on the Souchez road (we shall be returning to the village later on in the tour). Keeping a sharp look out on the right hand side of the road you should see a CWGC sign to the Sucrerie cemetery on the outskirts of the village. The cemetery is in fields behind buildings, and is not easily spotted from the road and it is necessary to walk a few hundred yards to reach it. Proceed to the southern end of the cemetery; in the fields at the edge of the wood to the south east were a number of houses known as the Mill Malon.

This was attacked by French troops coming down into the valley from the south on May 31st, who ejected the defenders. They then proceeded to go down a communication trench towards the sucrerie (a sugar refinery) which used to be approximately where a large complex now stands, to the east of the cemetery. By nightfall they had removed the enemy from their defences, but the Germans launched a successful counter-attack towards midnight, and pushed the French back into the

The village of Carency from Hill 125, both now in the hands of the French after the successful attack in May, 1915. Some 1,800 German Pioneers had turned the area into a formidable redoubt. Earthworks can be seen to the right of the picture.

communication trench. Reinforcements were brought up, using the cover of the bed of the stream and by the time night fell the position was in French hands, and was being consolidated. (The sucrerie is of historical interest for reasons other than military events. It is reputed to have been one of the first, if not the first, to produce the sugar substitute saccarine, manufactured from a by-product of coal tar, toluene, obviously in plentiful supply from the neighbouring mines.) Thus, at long last, the Lorette spur and the villages below it had been overcome. But now the French occupied inhospitable terrain, overlooked by the Germans from positions such as the Pimple (Hill119) to the east of Souchez. Indeed, one final attempt was made on June 16th to take Vimy Ridge; but the German defensive barrage caught the attacking French, and only the Moroccans were able to achieve their objective - Hill 119 which they were forced to give up as their position was far too vulnerable with the failure of their neighbouring divisions. On June 18th, Foch ended the Second Battle of Artois.

For the next few months the French pursued a policy of nibbling at the German line, and by the time of the opening of the Third Battle of

**Carieul Chateau today.**

Artois on September 25th they had brought the line forward so that the protagonists were separated by the Carency-Souchez railway line. The track bed may be seen on the right of the road; there is a drive to an imposing building, Carleul Chateau (on the modern map Carieul) , and immediately beside it a turning to the south. It is possible to drive in here and stop to survey the ground. The chateau was attacked on September 25th (when the British were launching their attack a few miles away,

26

at Loos) by members of the *chasseurs alpins*. The Germans had fortified the park in their usual efficient and effective way, and had added to the difficulty of an assault by breaking the banks of the stream and thereby creating a great morass. Despite all this, the French broke through and were able to occupy the western part of Souchez, assisted by the relative success of the troops attacking to the north of them. However, success did not come to those attacking Souchez from the south.

**Proceed** to the centre of Souchez and turn left; the itinerary will bring us back to the village to complete this part of the French front later in the tour.

Arriving at the top of the hill to the north of the village, take the signposted left turn to Notre Dame de Lorette. There is quite a steep climb to the top, where the road comes to a plateau and the vast French National Cemetery. Drive all the way around the cemetery and you will come to a number of buildings where there is a first rate museum, with an excellent display of equipment and uniforms, as well as a series of very effective, life-size dioramas, complete with an English commentary. A new extensive French park has been opened alongside. A visit to the museum must not be missed and will take up to half an hour. Near to the museum is a large cafe; although the main hall is not very prepossessing, there is a pleasant restaurant attached, and this makes an excellent spot to stop and recover.

In the cemetery there are about 20,000 burials, and another 20,000 or so buried in the ossuaries surmounted by the tower. The Basilica was erected by the then Bishop of Arras and he is now buried in it. It was due to his energy that this National cemetery was established here - the Artois equivalent of the one at Verdun. That too was created as a consequence of pressure co-ordinated by a Bishop, in this case of Verdun. The basilica has a mass celebrated in it every Sunday at 11 am and a short ceremony of remembrance follows outside afterwards. The

**The main street of the village of Carency, the houses of which had been turned into a virtual labyrinth of blockhouses with connecting trenches, by the occupying Germans. The French took it back in their May offensive.**

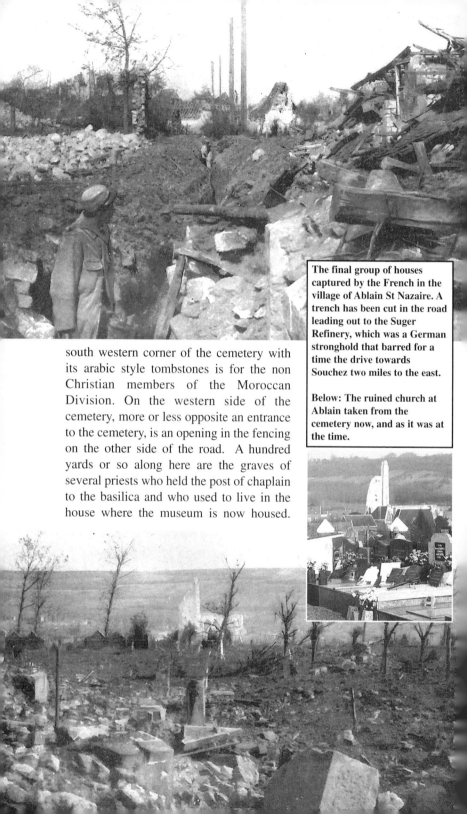

south western corner of the cemetery with its arabic style tombstones is for the non Christian members of the Moroccan Division. On the western side of the cemetery, more or less opposite an entrance to the cemetery, is an opening in the fencing on the other side of the road. A hundred yards or so along here are the graves of several priests who held the post of chaplain to the basilica and who used to live in the house where the museum is now housed.

Ablain St Nazaire from the Carency Road. Note the French Ossuary (the tower on the skyline) in the cemetery of Notre Dame De Lorette, and the ruined church of Ablain (far right).

Jews are buried amongst the rest, but with a star of David as opposed to a cross.

The energetic should take the opportunity of climbing the stairs of the lighthouse tower, standing some 170 feet high. There are spectacular views across the country, although much of the ground that is covered by this tour is hidden by the steep banks of the Lorette spur. The Lorette memorial is visible from the Messines Ridge, just south of the Ypres Salient some thirty miles or more to the north.

**Return to the car** and drive back to the main entrance to the cemetery on the south side. On entering the cemetery, to the right, is a stone marking the site of the original chapel. There was an oratory erected here by the artist, Florent Guilbert, in 1727, in thanksgiving for recovery from an illness. He ascribed this recovery to his participation

Ruined Church of Ablain St Nazaire

Spur of the White Way

French National Cemetery Notre Dame De Lorette

Sucrerie British Cemetery

Site of the Sucrerie

in a pilgrimage to the Marian shrine of Loretto in Italy. The oratory was destroyed in the French Revolution, but was rebuilt in 1815 and then embellished by an enthusiastic Parish Priest in the 1870s. By the time of the outbreak of the war the little church attracted a steady flow of pilgrims. At the time of the attack on May 9th the chapel was about a kilometre from the French front line.

For much of 1915 the French had steadily worked their way eastwards along the Lorette hill and by the end of April 1915 three of the five spurs that were on the south side had been captured. The Germans had spent their time since occupying the hill making their positions as strong as possible - several lines of trenches reinforced with concrete and earthworks, redoubts that could provide flanking fire when trench lines were lost, and a considerable fortification that was situated towards the eastern edge of the cemetery which included tunnel systems some fifty feet deep.

**See Map page 15** In the initial dash on May 9th, the *chasseurs alpins* managed to overrun three lines of trenches but the Germans were able to bring fire to bear on the attacking French from several quarters - from Ablain St Nazaire to the south, from Souchez to the east and from artillery hidden away in Angres. The future of the ground of Lorette was presaged by the use of a vast mine crater just in front of the new French line as an enormous burial ground.

> 'It is hot, and the smell is atrocious. The dead of the previous months, with only the thinnest covering of mud over them, have been torn from their graves by the shells. The plateau is a charnel house.'

On May 12th the chapel and most of the rest of the plateau fell into

Ruins of the Sucrerie at Ablain where fierce fighting took place as the Germans tried to stem the fierce onslaught on their positions in May, 1915. In the middle distance smoke rises from fires in the village.

**German shelters in the neighbourhood of Souchez showing signs of shrapnel damage to the corrugated iron.**

French hands; a few remnants from the chapel and memorabilia and letters of the troops will be found on one of the landings of the lighthouse. It was not until May 21st that the Spur of the White Way fell and thus almost all of the Lorette Hill.

To the south of the cemetery is a statue of General Maistre, whose XXI Corps was responsible for the capture of the feature. An orientation table is also nearby.

**Take the road back** towards the museum, but before following the road around to the north take the minor road on the left. This falls away steeply down the hill towards Ablain St Nazaire; to your right is the Spur of the White Way, over which so much blood was shed. Take the second road to the right, this will bring you out by the impressive ruins of the Church.

Before 1914 this had been a particularly fine church, built in the early years of the sixteenth century. The ruins are open for inspection, and are well worth a visit; it was here that the German garrison of the village fought its last desperate action. By 1270 Ablain was famous for its hospice under the protection of St Nazaire and attracted many pilgrims. The story has it that Louise, the daughter of the Prince of Bourbon was suddenly cured of madness induced by pains of love. In 1505 her father decided to build a new church at Ablain in thanksgiving, and employed as the architect Jacques Caron, who was responsible for the belfry of the town hall in Arras in the *Place des*

**Chasseurs alpins wait for the order to continue their advance, May 11th, 1915. The attack was in full swing when this photograph was taken in front of the German positions at Neuville-Souchez.**

*Heros.* The bell tower was built in the traditional Gothic style and was 43 metres high; the rest of the building was in flamboyant Gothic.

**Take the road to Souchez**; on arrival turn right and follow the D937 towards Arras. The road goes up a hill; keep to the right and turn right into a small road leading to the communal cemetery. This approach is marked by the statue of General Barbot, commander of 77 Division. He was killed on the evening of May 10th famously uttering, as he was dying, 'Beautiful ...glorious day...victory.' He is now buried at Notre Dame de Lorette. His division had performed wonders in the early moments of the opening of the attack on May 9th, carrying all before it. It captured Hill 119 (the Pimple) on its right, had troops in the centre

**French National Cemetery at Notre Dame De Lorette**

Chaplains' Cemetery

Moroccan graves

Basilica of Notre Dame De Lorette

Museum and Restaurant area

Ossuary and Light Tower

Commemorative Plaque of original chapel

Statue of General Maistre, XXI Corps Commander

of Souchez, but was held up by flanking fire from Carency on its left. By the end of that day, however, it was forced back from much of the captured ground for lack of reinforcements. They had advanced almost three miles and broken through a complex series of defences to open fields beyond. Despite the disappointment, some substantial gains had been made, albeit leaving them under direct German observation. Hill 119 is clearly visible from the cemetery, over to the east, an area of open field to the right of a wood.

General Barbot

As an aside, when I first visited the battlefields I thought that the statue of General Barbot was to some Reformation Evangelical preacher. In fact he is wearing the distinctive beret of the *chasseurs alpins*, among the fiercest of French fighting troops, with an awesome reputation. From mid 1915 onwards the French were to adopt a steel helmet, the *casque Adrian*, its distinctive shape based on a fireman's helmet.

By the end of June 1915 most of Souchez was still in German hands, with the French lapping at the edges. On September 25th 1915, some hours after the British had launched their Loos offensive, the French attacked Souchez and Hill 119 and, although the cemetery was once more captured (as it had been several times earlier in the year), they were forced to evacuate it and other gains in the area. However, on September 26th the village - or, rather, its site, fell into French hands and the Germans withdrew to their second line positions. The offensive was closed down, effectively, on September 28th, although fighting continued in the Souchez sector, gaining the French a substantial footing in Givenchy Wood and a tenable, though exposed, position on the western slopes of Hill119 and Vimy Ridge, beyond Neuville St Vaast.

The track in front of the cemetery leads south westwards, and offers good views over the May and June fighting, as well as the general approach of Barbot's men on May 9th.

**Continuing south** the British cemetery of Cabaret Rouge is on the right. The Cabaret Rouge was a building on the other side of the road, further back towards Souchez. It was captured on May 9th and it was along the Chemin des Pylones, (later known to the British as the Music Hall Line) a track running north - south some two hundred yards to the east of Cabaret Rouge that the men of the 77th Division (known as *La Division Barbot*) found themselves on the evening of that day. The

Divisional historian wrote:

> 'The trees along the Bethune road were gradually cut to pieces by the shells, and the Cabaret Rouge fell down.
>
> 'The survivors of the French attack, who had no time to dig themselves in deeply, lay on the ground behind slight ridges of earth, which afforded little protection against the splinters. The number of the wounded increased with disconcerting rapidity, but they were forced to stay where they were, among the *Tirailleurs* [sharpshooters], as the barrage prevented any movement being made to the rear.The field kitchens could not reach the men, whose water bottles were empty. The heat was suffocating on the arid plateau and the men, mad with thirst, drank their own water.'

It was the line of this track until a few hundred yards north of Neuville St Vaast that indicated the limits of French success in this sector. The result of the September attack was to move the French front into the valley below, still called Zouave Valley after the heroic actions of these troops in the 1915 fighting. Cabaret Rouge became a mortuary dump:

> 'Each night in front of the Cabaret Rouge the dead were loaded on carts, while the companies going up the line passed by long rows of other dead awaiting their turn to be removed.'

**Proceeding southwards**, the Czech cemetery and memorials to the Polish and Czech members of the Foreign Legion will be found alongside. These memorials, in particular, commemorate their actions on May 9th.

This completes this short circuit of some of the activities of the French army in this sector. In 1915 this small part of France had seen some of the bloodiest offensive action by the French (a distinction shared with the Champagne). Lessons had been learned; questions had been raised - the use of artillery, the placement of reserves, and the possibility of breaking well entrenched position with rapidity, but also of being broken before them. The Germans had shown themselves to be great masters of fighting defensive trench warfare. The French had shown what could be achieved by troops of high morale and well motivated. For example, the French had learned the vital importance of ensuring that clearing parties were part of the attacking waves, whose chief responsibility was to ensure that no pockets of Germans remained in dug outs to attack troops from the rear. This lesson was not so readily learned by the other protagonists. However despite the valour and elan of these onslaughts of 1915, the year was one of disappointment for allied arms.

## Bibliography

*The Times History of the War* Vol VI.

*Michelin Guide to the battlefields: ARRAS.* Reprinted 1995 and available from David Harrison, bookseller, 16 Conway Road, West Wimbledon, London SW20 8PA; and from Naval and Military Press, Heathfield, East Sussex. Tel. 01435 830111. It is an excellent guide, written in the immediate post war years.

*Field Marshal Sir Henry Wilson: His Life and Diaries.* Maj Gen Sir CE Callwell. Cassell, 1927.

*Les Carnets de guerre de Louis Barthas, tonnelier. 1914 - 1918.* Editions la decouverte, 1992.

Souchex Cemetery then and now.

# Chapter Two

## THE BRITISH ARRIVE: MINING OPERATIONS AND TRENCH RAIDS, MARCH - MAY 1916

The timing of the arrival of the British Army in this sector was determined by the opening of the German Offensive at Verdun on February 21st 1916; within a day the French command realised that the attack was no limited adventure, and potentially could be serious. The Germans had also launched a diversionary attack on Hill 119, the Pimple, on that day, and pushed the French off the summit and back down the west side of the ridge. Joffre asked the British at first to relieve two corps on the Tenth Army Front to enable him to form a reserve force; and shortly after this he asked for the relief of the other two corps forming the Tenth Army. To these requests Haig agreed with alacrity (indeed, the offer was originally made some days earlier, when a German attack at Verdun was first rumoured). On March 1st the Fourth Army, under Rawlinson, came into existence, taking over the Somme Front. This left Allenby's Third Army holding the front from just south of Souchez to south of Hebuterne. This transfer was completed by 14th March.

1915 had been a year in which mining operations, as a routine part of trench warfare on the Western Front, had reached a degree of intensity which continued until the early summer of 1916. Mines were used as part of a general offensive (for example their use at Carency on May 9th) but more often they were used for highly localised attacks.

**In February 1916 the British Army took over the sector of the front line north of Arras, thus relieving pressure on the French, who had just entered into the fighting around Verdun.**

These attacks often had the objective of securing a particularly valuable piece of ground, offering good views over the enemy lines, and thereby denying a similar advantage to the foe. Examples of this form of warfare can be found around the Ypres Salient (eg Hooge, Bellewaarde Ridge, the Bluff and Hill 60) and further south on the British front at Givenchy and around Loos - and all this only in the British sector. Mines were sometimes blown to provide the basis of an earthwork which could be fortified and manned and thereby dominate a particular part of the line or of No Man's Land. Sometimes they were simply blown to create an obstruction to the enemy's view.

The new sector at which the British had arrived was admirably suited to this form of warfare. Underground working also opened up further possibilities. Once the nature of the ground around Arras was established, it became clear that extensive tunnelling and adaptation of existing excavations could provide both secure shelter and communications from the rear areas to the Front Line.

For the British to make use of this situation they required skilled tunnellers. The need for a specialist battalion for both mining and sapping had been recognised as far back as December 1914, when Rawlinson asked for such a unit. There were problems with this request. The rather haphazard way that characterised the British Army's need to adapt to changing circumstances and because of the huge demands made upon the resources of the Royal Engineers, and because of the volunteer and chaotic arrangements for expanding the army, such suitable men had to be recruited from troops already serving in other branches of the army. By February 1915 it had been decided to create specialist Tunnelling Companies - eight initially, twenty five by mid 1916 along with seven provided from the Dominions. These each consisted of some three hundred men (though some had over five hundred, which increase allowed for unskilled labourers), with experienced mining engineers being recruited in due course as officers.

The original demand was for 'clay kickers', men who were capable of working in cramped and difficult conditions. There were large numbers of men in this trade, who were used to excavating tunnels for sewers and latterly electrical cables and water pipes. Their skills were ideal for what was then required at the front - the making of small tunnels which could be driven quite rapidly under the German lines, the excavation of a chamber at the end and the firing of a mine.

The British therefore arrived on this part of the front reasonably prepared to face a considerable mining challenge. Both they and the infantry had to face two particular problem areas on the Ridge, however. The loss of the crest of the Pimple to the Germans' surprise

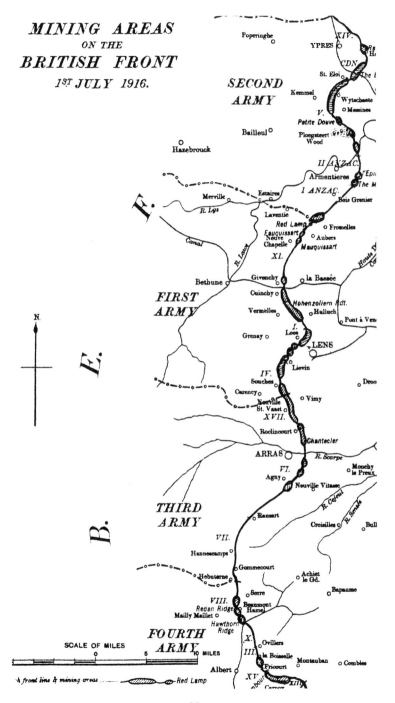

MINING AREAS
ON THE
BRITISH FRONT
1ST JULY 1916.

SECOND
ARMY

FIRST
ARMY

THIRD
ARMY

FOURTH
ARMY

N.

E.

B.

F.

Poperinghe

YPRES

XIV.

CDN

St. Eloi

The I

Kemmel

Wytschaete

Messines

V.

Petite Douve

Ploegsteert
Wood

Bailleul

II ANZAC.

Hazebrouck

Armentieres

'Epii

The M

I ANZAC

Bois Grenier

Merville

Estaires

Laventie

R. Lys

Red Lamp

Fromelles

Fauquissart

Aubers

Neuve
Chapelle

Mauquissart

Canal

XI.

R. Loire

Givenchy

la Bassée

Bethune

Cuinchy

Hohenzollern Rdt.

Vermelles

Hulluch

Pont à Ven

Haute D

Grenay

I.
Loos

LENS

IV.

Lievin

Souchez

Droo

Carency

Vimy

Neuville
St. Vaast

XVII.

Roclincourt

Chantecler

ARRAS

R. Scarpe

Monchy
le Preux

VI.

Agny

Neuville Vitasse

N.

R. Cojeul

R. Sensée

THIRD
ARMY

Ransart

Croisailles

Bull

VII.

Hannescamps

Gommecourt

Achiet
le Gd.

Bapaume

Hebuterne

Serre

VIII.

Redan Ridge

Beaumont
Hamel

Mailly Maillet

Hawthorn
Ridge

SCALE OF MILES

0        5        10 MILES

MILES

X.

Ovillers

III.

la Boisselle

Montauban

Combles

Albert

Fricourt

XV.

h front line & mining areas ........ ⬛⬛⬛ ⬛ Red Lamp

39

Clay-kicking was a technique of digging tunnels developed in peacetime for constructing sewers etc, and proved useful in operations on the Western Front. Flanders was ideal for clay-kickers, who speedily drove tunnels under the German lines. In Arras only the first few feet were clay; therefore miners were required. On the left is the special 'grafting' spade and on the right what was known as the 'cross'.

attack of February 21st removed the allies from their only high point on the ridge. It also lost the French front line trench system and forced the new British arrivals to take up often ill-defined and certainly unsatisfactory former second line positions as their new front line. Circumstances were made even more trying by the steep drop down to Zouave valley, on the other side of which lay the reserve and transport lines. An earlier attack by the Germans, on February 8th, had removed the French from their positions for about a kilometre south of Central Avenue. Many of the earlier days of the British occupation of the sector had the Tunnellers concerned primarily with defensive operations.

## Territorials holding the Line

The 46th (North Midland) Division arrived on this new front for the British Army in the early days of March 1916. Amongst the battalions of the division were two from the Leicestershire Regiment, the 1/4th and 1/5th. These had both suffered grievously in an attack on October 13th 1915 on the Hohenzollern Redoubt, in the Loos sector, most particularly the 1/4th Leicesters. They lost, in the one day, all twenty officers who took part in the attack and 453 other ranks; 188 NCOs and men answered the rollcall.

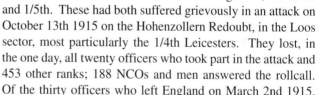

Of the thirty officers who left England on March 2nd 1915, only two remained. The 1/5th Leicesters, who were in reserve on that fateful day, lost in casualties ten officers and 177 other ranks. The New Year had brought better news, as the division was ordered to proceed to the Mediterranean and on January 21st 1916 the two battalions were on board the former Cunarder, HMT *Aldania*. The 1/4th Leicesters' history describes the period of awaiting embarkation at Marseilles as one of happiness.

'There is one period of the battalion's sojourn in France which will ever remain the most fragrant of its memories. It is the time spent at Marseilles. From a "bloody war" it became not a "good war" but a "lovely war".'

There were stewards on board and the officers all had comfortable cabins and the men bunks. Food was good, hot and plentiful. 'It almost seemed too good to last. It was.' The following morning the battalions disembarked, as the order for Egypt had been cancelled, and although they did not know it, the Gallipoli adventure was being abandoned. The division went off to refit and, amongst other new items of military hardware, received their first issues of Lewis Guns (two per company) and 'tin hats', the first with great joy, the latter with some suspicion.

Initial instructions had the division moving to the Somme, taking over the line around Beaumont Hamel; in the event, they were moved towards Arras, arriving at Villers au Bois on March 8th and went into the line on March 9th. The intention was to make the relief of the French as secret an event as possible, even down to sending in advance parties in French helmets. The effort was wasted; on March 7th, two days before the relief, a French listening post reported that a German patrol had looked in and were heard to comment that the British had not yet arrived. It was to bring about a change in the nature of the warfare; the French and the Germans had for some time adopted a 'live and let live' approach to their daily existence, though of course the recent local offensives had jolted both sides.

The line taken over by 1/5th Leicesters ran from Ersatz Avenue in the north to Vincent Street in the south (at the time they still had French See map on page 43 names, for example *Boyau* [trench] *d'Ersatz*). As the trenches had escaped the recent German attack they were sound enough but very dirty. In the process of the handover, the newcomers had not been informed of the continuing presence of two companies of French engineers. This almost led to unfortunate casualties amongst the French, who were in danger of being shot by their British allies. Indeed, this holding of the line by two nationalities almost led to lethal confusion when a French engineer, soon after midnight, was observed running around the lines gesticulating and uttering warnings about a mine that was due to go off in half an hour. After some delay he was taken to the battalion headquarters, where it became clearer that the blast was to be a camouflet. The line was cleared locally, and the charge fired at 5 am. A huge crater was formed, which must have taken the German mine with it; a short tussle followed for the crater (an honourable draw) and the Battalion was left with the usual consequence of such an action - rebuilding a destroyed length of parapet.

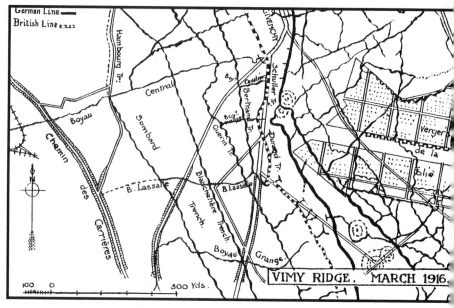

**Berthonval plus P Sector - The Sherwood Foresters' sector.**

Supplies were brought up to the line from Mont St Eloi on a narrow-gauge railway, using mule drawn trucks. This line came through to the *Talus des Zouaves* (Zouave Embankment) and the contents of the trucks were offloaded in a central dump. As the war progressed the dump and the offloading of the trucks was moved underground, but even before this it was a relatively secure place, shielded as it was by the steep bank of the valley. The journey over open plains to and from Mont St Eloi was never pleasant, and it was the norm that several of the mules would become casualties in the course of their run. The return run often took corpses for burial, a matter discussed further in the entry on Ecoivres Military Cemetery.

The time in the sector enabled both the Leicester battalions to recover from the traumatic losses at the Hohenzollern Redoubt the previous year, and during this period there were frequent arrivals of new drafts. However when the line was first taken over both battalions were severely under strength meaning that time in the trenches had to be extended. Not until early April were they strong enough to hold the line with only two companies instead of three. March brought alternating rain and snow, thaws and frost. The consequences for the trenches were severe - they crumbled and collapsed, and the communication trenches, which had to be well maintained as well, were particularly long. Many of the men had to hold their positions standing ankle deep in water and with little protection against the

42

elements. The situation was not helped by the fact that many of the men had spent some weeks sunning themselves in the south of France, and were therefore not hardened for the rigours of icy winter. Pneumonia and trench feet and fever were common - at one time twenty men or so of 1/5th Leicesters had to crawl on their hands and knees to their Aid Post because of the appalling state of their feet.

There were further demands that made life in Vimy hard; 'for sheer discomfort Vimy took a lot of beating', as the 1/4th Leicesters history comments. Hard work was put into restoring the parapets and parados - filling sandbags with sodden earth, helping to disperse spoil from the mines and draining the trenches. All the hard work was frequently destroyed by the arrival of German minenwerfers, better known as 'rum jars'. As they moved so slowly through the air they were easily spotted and avoided, however they caused immense damage to the trenches, each one destroying a length of ten yards or more.

The Germans also had the advantage when it came to sniping as it was the German custom to leave their snipers in one part of the front who thereby gained full knowledge of the terrain and the vulnerable points of the line opposite. There was a continual trickle of casualties because of this - the 1/4th Leicesters lost 2/Lt SF Lennard, commissioned recently from the ranks, to such a sniper.

The other great fear was the threat of mines being exploded under the trenches. The geophone had only been made recently available, and was still somewhat clumsy. When it did come into regular service it made the detection and accurate mapping of enemy mining operations (and, indeed, listening to conversation on occasions) possible and therefore improved the prediction of mine attacks and the taking of counter-measures. Because of this threat of attack from below, lines were sometimes held thinly or even moved in anticipation. A new line would be dug which the Germans would then attack ferociously with

Section of trench map of Vimy Edition 8A Sheet 44A S.W.3. Trenches corrected to 10.2.1917.

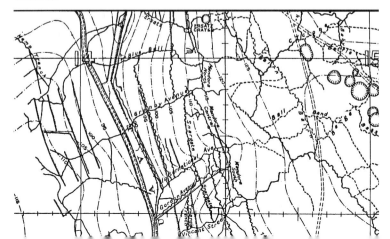

trench mortars. The British had only recently begun to get a reasonably effective weapon with which to respond, the Stokes Mortar. Thus when the 1/4th Lincolns decided to create a new line a few yards to the rear of the front line for fear of a mine being set off, the Germans set about the destruction of the line with ruthless ferocity. It was in this bombardment that Captain Roland Farmer, commanding C Company in the line north of Vincent Street, was killed, his body being blown out of the trenches and undiscovered for several hours.

'He was perhaps the quietest, certainly the bravest, officer of his time, for he feared nothing, and nothing could shake his calm, while it was said of him that he was never angry and never despondent. When he was killed, C Company lost their leader, and every man his best friend, while the mess lost one who was the most cheerful comrade of every officer.'

(*1/5th Leicesters* history). The sound of mines being exploded was part of everyday existence. On the other hand it was something to which no-one could become used, and of course morale suffered when tappings were heard - or even thought to be heard. It would take a strange person to be nonchalant at the prospect of being buried alive at any moment.

The commander of 138 Brigade, Brigadier General GC Kemp, was a former Royal Engineer. and keen on improving the strength and siting of his trenches. There was not much that could be done about the mines, as these were, for the time being, the responsibility of French engineers. Kemp frequently went out at night with a small party in and around No Man's Land to mark out new positions, the sites being pegged and outlined with lime. The fact was that for the most part 138 Brigade spent its time holding the line as best they could, in a sector where the Germans held the upper hand, and were also far better equipped for trench warfare. British inadequacy, indeed amateurism, in this area is well illustrated in the account of the activities of the battalion grenadiers in 1/5th Leicesters history.

**Captain Roland Farmer**
**1/5 Leicesters**

44

'The Battalion Grenadiers.....particularly enjoyed themselves, and their dug-out in the valley became a regular anarchists' arsenal. Fiendish missiles were made out of empty bottles stuffed with ammonal and other explosives, which they managed to obtain in large quantities from the French miners, while the strength of various poisons and gases was tested against the rats, against whose habitation they carried on an endless war. A catapult was erected for practice purposes, and our bombers became adept in its use, knowing exactly how much fuse to attach to a TNT-filled glass beer bottle to make it burst two seconds after landing in the Boche trench.'

**Primitive grenades were constructed from tin cans and bottles filled with TNT and a short piece of fuse wire attached. Bottom: Various contraptions were invented to propel the bombs towards the German trenches, with varying degrees of success.**

The tour of 46th Division was to end on April 20th; it was to be withdrawn in preparation for its tragic part in the Somme battle. In the last weeks the old communication trench *Boyau* 1, 2, 3, which had not been used by the British because of its poor state, had been re-dug and renamed Wortley Avenue after the Major General commanding the division. This alternative communication trench had become a necessity as *Ersatz* Avenue was coming under persistent and effective shell fire. The frequency of mine explosions had also increased. British tunnelling companies which were gradually replacing the French had determined that the only way to pre-empt the Germans was to blast mines as soon as possible.

The last three weeks of April and the first three of May witnessed a frenzy of underground fighting, mine and counter-mine following each other with bewildering speed and stupefying effect. The last days of 138 Brigade were spent in repairing damage caused to trenches by the mine blasts, fighting off German bombing attacks as they tried to occupy the western edge of the new crater lips and helping the miners with the provision of manual labour in their task. Indeed this task of assisting with the shovel continued even after the formal relief had taken place on April 20th. 1/4th Lincolns had been badly caught by a German mine, they lost many of their men and had a hundred yards or so of their front line demolished. D Company of 1/5th Leicesters had to stay in the line and help to repair the mess. So adept did some men show themselves as miners that twenty five of them were left behind to help the tunnellers - and most never rejoined the battalion being absorbed into the Engineers.

**Struggling to capture and hold the lip of a newly formed crater.**

The reason that mine warfare had again become so bitter seems, in part, to be due to the fact that the German shafts were catching up with the gains made by their infantry in the attacks of February. XVII Corps commander, Lieutenant General Julian Byng, was deeply concerned;

not only that all this activity might presage a German attack, but also at the effect the anxiety was having on the morale of his men. Tension was also high between tunneller officers and the battalions under which they worked - the tunnellers were under strict orders not to give away intelligence about what was happening - and was likely to happen - under the ground.

At 8.30 pm on May 15th 1916, 182 Tunnelling Company fired a series of mines under the German positions. The main charges were under a German trench which connected a new (April 19th) crater and an older one some tens of yards away. To protect the infantry attack and to enable them to hold the new craters it was proposed to fire two further charges to the right, near to the German line. These were designed to produce large lips thereby screening the view of the Germans from the attack.

**A danger of tunnelling: naturally produced noxious gasses could be released into the workings.**

The attack had to be carefully planned. Infantry came from 11/Lancs Fusiliers who attacked the craters on the right and 9/Loyal North Lancs who attacked those on the left and digging parties had to be provided to assist specialist pioneers and engineers. The artillery engaged in counter-battery fire just before the mines were exploded. The attack on the left craters went well, but elsewhere some of the infantry got too close and were buried in the debris from the explosion. Four officers from 11/Lancs Fusiliers were killed in the raid 2/Lts AK McFarlane, WF Baker, EL Jewell and R Barrett. Like the other officer fatalities mentioned above, they are buried in Ecoivres Military Cemetery. The new group of craters were named the Crosbie Craters - in honour of the Fusiliers' battalion CO, who at the time was temporarily commanding 74 Brigade.

See Map page 152

This attack and one some days earlier to the north had involved the creation of the massive Momber group of craters (Momber, Love and Kennedy), and was to have severe consequences. The British were showing themselves adept at the procedure of not only firing but also holding such craters. The German retaliation was to be swift and most effective, as shown in the following chapter.

### The Robin Hoods

To the right of 138 Brigade was the sector held by 139 Brigade, known as the Sherwood Forester Brigade. One of its battalions, the 1/7th Sherwood Foresters (the Notts and Derbyshire Regt) carried the

See Map
page 42

nickname 'the Robin Hoods'; this was unofficially carried over to the Brigade. 1/7th and 1/8th Sherwood Foresters held the left sector of their brigade front. They had a very similar experience in the trenches as their Midland neighbours to the right. The handover from the French was complicated by the fact that the ability to speak each other's language was limited in the extreme, and the situation was only saved from farce because one of the French officers had lived in London for fourteen years before the war. Perhaps nothing better indicates the speed with which the replacement of the French 10th Army was carried out than this extremely haphazard approach to dealing with what would be inevitable language problems in a sector which was under such considerable danger of attack.

**Detail from 1:5000 Map no date (probably Spring 1917) entitled Souchez River. The area around Kennedy Crater.**

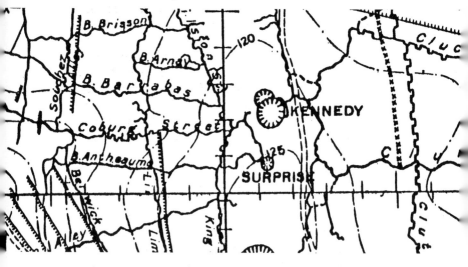

The sector covered by the battalions lay between *Boyau Central* (in due course Central Avenue) and *Boyau Lassalle* (later Lassalle Avenue). The front line had been shifted westwards some yards by the German attack of February 21st and the French hardly had time to settle down in the new position, the old second line trenches, which were in an indifferent state of repair. It was known that the German miners were pushing forward rapidly, and indeed already had one sap under the new front line. The French had proposed to set about a new defensive system, and the British immediately began constructing a strong second line trench (*Guerin*) some hundred yards or so to the west of *Schuler* and *Durand* Trenches, the existing front line. The problems were compounded by the excellent observation and sniping positions that the Germans had from the lips of a number of craters in No Man's Land - many parts of the communication trenches were clearly in their view.

See Map page 42

Problems of snipers, mortars and mining dominated the time in the trenches. Mining was the one that seemed to be the most urgent, and amongst other decisions made by the commanding officers was one to run two new communication trenches from *Guerin* to the front line. These were named 'Birkin' and 'Broadmarsh', the latter to become infamous in the coming months. A set of standing orders in the event of the Germans setting a mine were issued.

See Map page 67

''Secret: Action to be taken in case of mine explosion on front of Battalion holding left sector.

1. In the event of a crater being formed by enemy's mine explosion at any point of our front line, the near lip of the crater will be immediately occupied, and should the enemy have gained a footing in any part of our line, he will be ejected by bayonet and grenades.

2. The Company commander in the trench affected will at once take the following steps:- i. Send message to Artillery. "mine blown up opposite. Please give covering fire, also send report to Battalion Headquarters." ii. Send covering party half platoon to hold near lip. iii. Send digging party of half platoon which will draw tools and materials stored in the special dump which contains 1000 sandbags, 25 shovels, 5 picks, 2 rolls barbed wire, 40 corkscrew stakes and wire palisades. 1v. Send two parties of four grenadiers each, to protect each side of flank digging party. v. Independent flanking parties will be sent out by OC Company concerned, as verbally detailed, in the event of explosion at one of the specified places, each party consisting of 1 Lewis Gun contingent, 2 Rifle Grenadiers, 4 Grenadiers and 12 Rifles under one Commander vi. Bring up Support. vii. Send constant

information to Battalion Headquarters. viii. Place a post on main communicating trenches to prevent stragglers from getting to the rear.

3. Battalion Headquarters will, if necessary, fill the place of troops moved forward from support trench by sending forward a Company from the Reserve Battalion.'

A life of hardship in such a precarious position had few lighter moments. Some of the more senior NCOs became 'time expired' (under their conditions of service as Territorials) and were able to return home. Some might have found humour in the dug-outs that the French had occupied, many of which had their walls decorated; battalion headquarters boasted drawings of ballet girls beautifully drawn on the boarding of the walls with poker work and chalk. At least there was rather more comfort in the billets at Berthonval Farm, where huge caverns were equipped with bunk beds. Billets at Mont St Eloi - of wooden huts or tents - were rather less acceptable. One staff officer made himself particularly popular by employing a small army of French women to operate a laundry. By such small considerations could life be made, if only barely, tolerable.

The Robin Hood Brigade left the sector on April 30th, their place being taken by units filling in from either flank. The 46th Division was en route for the Somme.

## Bibliography

*History of the 7th Battalion Sherwood Forester 1914 - 1918.* Lt Col A Brewill. J & H Bell 1921.

*The Sherwood Foresters in the Great War, 1914 - 1919: 1/8th Battalion.* Capt WC Weetman. Thos Forman & Sons 1920.

*History of the Lancashire Fusiliers 1914 - 1918, Volume 1.* Maj Gen JC Latter. Gale and Polden 1949.

*The Lancashire Fusiliers Annual.* Article by Capt J Metcalfe 11/Lancs Fus.

*Footprints of the 1/4th Leicestershire Regiment.* John Milne. Edgar Backus 1935.

*The Fifth Leicestershire Regiment 1914 - 1919.* Capt JD Hills. Echo Press 1919.

*Tunnellers.* Capt W Grant Grieve and B Newman. Herbert Jenkins 1936; reprinted Naval and Military Press 1995.

*War Underground.* A. Barrie. Frederick Muller Ltd. 1962

*Military Operations France and Belgium. 1915* Volumes 1 and 2. *1916* Volume 1. Compiled by Brig Gen Sir J Edmonds.

# Chapter Three

# A MINOR AFFAIR ON VIMY RIDGE

In many respects the circumstances surrounding the events on Vimy Ridge in May 1916 were highly unusual, even allowing for the many unpredictable turns that engagements took in the Great War. It is unfortunate that the construction of a motorway and the creation of the Memorial Park has served to remove many of the traces of battle and views of the ground as it then was, but it is still possible to have a worthwhile battleground tour over the remaining recognisable features.

The backdrop to the German attack of May 21st lay in the increasing success of the British Tunnelling Companies in asserting some degree of control over mining operations in an area where previously the Germans ruled supreme. This predominance had been achieved in large measure by the capture of a number of French mine shafts in the very limited attacks of February, thus ensuring that the Germans held the mining initiative.

The 47th (London) Division came into the line on March 16th holding the northern part of Vimy Ridge, the Souchez and Carency sectors. The British front here was divided into four sectors. The northernmost was **Souchez**, running north from the Pimple, including the eastern and southern slopes of the Lorette spur. To its right was **Carency** Sector, whose boundary with the **Berthonval** Sector was Central Avenue and to the south was **'P'** sector.

The early days of the Londoners at Vimy were quiet and relatively uneventful; trench mortars were a nuisance, but 18/London Regiment (Lond) went so far in these relaxed days as to give the enemy opposite a copy of *The Times*. The change in atmosphere was ascribed to the removal of a benign Saxon division, as well as the coming to fruition of German mining schemes. When 176 Tunnelling Company came on the scene, they found the German mining scheme well advanced, and could only engage in frantic defensive measures.

The tense situation was broken on April 26th by the blowing of a German mine, within a couple of hundred yards of the Pimple. The blowing of the mine was anticipated and the line had been largely evacuated, and although the front line was damaged by the blast, the British were able to secure and consolidate the near lip. The crater was dubbed 'New Cut'. Another German mine some hundred yards or so to the north was expected to be blown in the very near future, so the British fired a defensive camouflet mine, which in turn blew the

See Map page 53

German one creating the huge Broadbridge crater. The Germans retaliated by firing another mine between these two new craters, in effect joining them up. Accompanied by a heavy barrage this mine caused considerable casualties to 6/Lond. Under the leadership of their CO, Lt Col W Mildren, the battalion managed to retain control of the situation and restored the line through what now became known as Mildren Crater.

The situation near the Pimple may have been relieved from the immediate threat of further German attack from underground, but the same happy situation could not be said to apply to the line between Coburg Alley and Ersatz Alley. Some eleven German galleries were believed to be active in the area to which the only solution was to counter mine with great alacrity.

> 'The work was pushed on with all possible speed. Increased shifts of miners worked all night May 2nd-3rd, burrowing forward from old French listening galleries; large parties of the 141st Brigade brought up timber, and every available man from the trenches carried soil from the mine-shafts.'

Four mines were fired at 4.45pm on May 3rd and under covering artillery fire 21/Lond rushed forward to occupy the far side of the resulting three craters, one of the mines having failed to puncture the surface. Pioneers and Sappers then consolidated the near lips so that by dawn the forward infantry could be withdrawn to the new position. The craters were named Kennedy (after 21/Lond commander), Momber

**See Map page 48 and 152**

(commanding 176 Tunnelling Company) and Love (after the RE Field Company commander - this officer went on to win two DSOs in 1918). British offensive - or retaliatory - operations continued further south, with the blowing of the Crosbie craters on May 15th.

The 47th Division took over the Berthonval sector on May 19th, giving up the far cushier Souchez sector and Lorette defences to the 23rd Division. This was unfortunate, as the Londoners had no time to get some idea of their bearings before the Germans launched their strike on May 21st.

### The German Attack, May 21st 1916

The Germans had a new, albeit temporary, commander of their troops facing the British. General von Freytag-Loringhoven was Deputy Chief

**See Map page 179**

of the General Staff of the Supreme Command under Falkenhayn and previously to this he had been the senior liaison officer at the Austro-Hungarian Great Headquarters. On April 15th he petitioned to be allowed six weeks leave of absence to obtain experience of the front, and replaced the sick commander of the 17th Division which held the

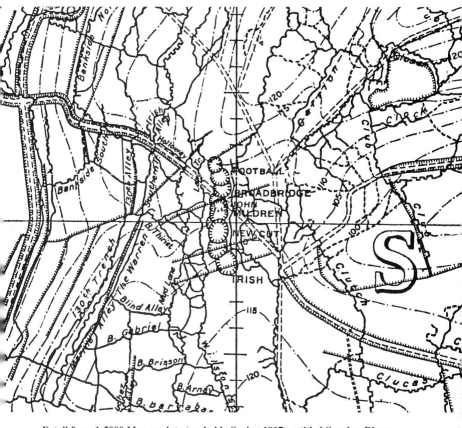

**Detail from 1:5000 Map no date (probably Spring 1917) entitled Souchez River.**

line in front of Givenchy en Gohelle. As chance had it the Corps Commander was also granted sick leave, so Freytag-Loringhoven took on that task also. His IX Reserve Corps now faced Lieut General Henry Wilson's IV Corps (or at least did so when that Corps sector shuffled south to the Central Avenue boundary on May 19th). The career of Wilson in many respects mirrored that of his opposite number - he, too had never commanded in battle before; indeed Wilson had never even commanded his own battalion, only a provisional affair for a year at the end of the Boer War. Wilson had been the Senior British Liaison Officer at the French GQG and had only gained his Corps at the end of December 1915. By the time he relinquished command on December 1st 1916 his Corps had not moved from Vimy Ridge and the only battle in which it engaged was this brief affair on May 21st. On leaving the Corps he returned to liaison duties and ended his war by being Chief of the Imperial General Staff. Freytag-Loringhoven, having stirred the hornets nest, returned to staff duties on May 31st.

When Freytag-Loringhoven arrived at his new command he soon realised that he had come to, "a windy corner of the Western front".

'The casualties which we suffered by mine explosions and continual night attacks aroused in me lively anxiety, which I communicated one day towards the end of April to the chief of the Corps staff and his GSO 1 [a senior staff officer]. Things could not go on as they were....If by attack we could throw back the British over the position which we had held until the end of September 1915 [ie before the French offensive of the 25th of that month] and so rob them of all their mine shafts, and hold the position won, we should have tranquillity.'

German regimental accounts back up the view of their new commander. Thus the 163rd Regimental history (which was serving in the sector where the mines of late April and early May had been fired) reports:

'These continual mine explosions in the end got on the nerves of the men. The posts in the front trenches and the garrisons of the dug-outs were always in danger of being buried alive. Even in the quietest night there was the dreadful feeling that in the next moment one might die a horrible and cruel death. One stood in the front line defenceless and powerless against these fearful mine explosions. Against all other fighting methods there was some protection. Against this kind of warfare, valour was of no avail, not even the greatest foresight. Running back, retirement were useless: like lightning from the clear heavens, like the sudden occurrence of some catastrophe of nature, these mine explosions took place. Some change must be brought about, the British mine shafts on Vimy Ridge must be captured.'

This view was shared by the 86th Regiment, whose sector included the Crosbie Craters:

'Our companies had suffered heavy losses through the British mine explosions. It was accepted that other large parts of our trench system were undermined and might fly into the air at any moment, and that some counter-measures must be devised. We could not fight the enemy any longer with his own weapons, for he was superior to us in both men and material. The commander therefore decided to assault the British front trenches, gain possession of the mine shafts, and thus bring underground warfare to an end for a considerable time.'

These German views of the British tunnellers are a considerable tribute

to them considering the very limited time they had to assert some sort of control over the situation underground, especially given the fact that so many of the workings of their French predecessors had been lost in February.

Before the German offensive opened up and soon after the British arrived, there had been moves to reorganise the line and move it westwards to a front running from Ecurie to Souchez. This would be far more tenable and less open to German observation and nagging trench mortar fire, as

**A well constructed German front line trench. One of the soldiers is holding the latest pattern stick grenade, introduced in 1915 - the 'tatty-masher'.**

the Germans would lose the safety of the steep eastern side of the ridge in which to conceal these weapons in relative safety. Haig was not in principle against the idea - anything to avoid enmeshing divisions and artillery which were being nurtured and gathered for the forthcoming Big Push on the Somme. But although such a move made military sense, it did not make political sense, for the French had gained that ground with much of her blood. Political necessity, as was often the case (and undoubtedly still is) over-ruled military considerations. The British had to stay where they were and make the best of it.

Freytag-Loringhoven got the consent of his Army Commander (Sixth Army, under Crown Prince Ruprecht of Bavaria) for his limited operation. Doubtless he was able to use the influence of his usual appointment to procure all that he would require - and above all that included heavy artillery and the ammunition to go with it.

The German preparations continued. British intelligence considered that the enemy was too preoccupied with events around Verdun where the battle was reaching a crescendo and on the Eastern Front where the enormously successful Russian Offensive under Brusilov was about to be launched for them to consider a further attack on the Western Front. Despite the misgivings of the officers on the ground, and in the light of negative intelligence from the air (although operations had been severely limited because of the

**Crown Prince Ruprecht of Bavaria**

weather) the process of thinning out the various British Armies to build up the Fourth commenced in May,

The German onslaught was to fall principally upon the Berthonval sector and it was at this very point that the most disruptive command change imaginable took place on the night of May 19th/20th. Army command changed (from Third to First); Corps command changed (from XVII to IV); Divisional command changed (from 25 to 47) - and with it all the complications that arose over channels of command, artillery cover and a host of other logistical problems. Whilst this transfer had been taking place the Germans had been engaged upon a systematic artillery programme, registering their guns on communications trenches and British artillery positions. At 3 pm on May 21st the bombardment proper began to fall from Love Crater in the north to Broadmarsh Crater (heading Royal Avenue) in the south. It **See Map** extended to the rear as well to Zouave Valley preventing immediate **opposite** reinforcements being brought up and to disrupt communication to the **and on** battery positions; to Chateau de la Haie (47th Division headquarters) **page 152** and to the billeting villages round and about. Amongst the usual heavy explosive shells were numbers of tear gas shells. The bombardment was unprecedented in the eyes of many observers - there were eighty batteries firing on a front of just over a mile and each had an average allocation of two hundred shells per hour. The front under attack, and much of the ground to the rear, was completely lost in clouds of dust, smoke and gas.

The German advance started at 7.45 pm, and for the most part they were able to make easy progress as the British lines had been all but obliterated. On the right the British were forced back to the road running at the base of the *Talus des Zouaves*. Sappers took the precaution of manning the defences before Cabaret Rouge on the west side of the valley. The situation was one of confusion - but at least the line about Broadmarsh was secured, and the Germans had made relatively little progress north of Momber crater. An ill-considered counter-attack was launched at 2 am and achieved nothing, although the line on the left of the German attack was partially restored by the 8/Loyal North Lancs (Loyals). Once the new line had been ascertained, Wilson was all for launching a new counter attack, but this was vetoed by Haig, unless it had been properly prepared. An attack on the 23rd soon broke down and in the end the British learned to live with the situation, especially as it became clear from aerial reconnaissance that this was a local attack and not a full blooded affair to capture Arras as Allenby, commanding Third Army, at one time feared. Unsatisfactory though the new position might be, Haig did not consider it untenable,

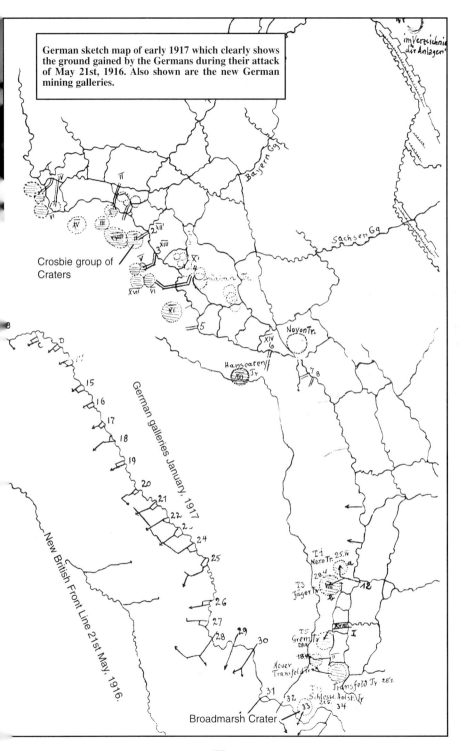

German sketch map of early 1917 which clearly shows the ground gained by the Germans during their attack of May 21st, 1916. Also shown are the new German mining galleries.

Crosbie group of Craters

German galleries January, 1917

New British Front Line 21st May, 1916.

Broadmarsh Crater

and the only alternative - a full blooded offensive with all that that entailed - could only detract from plans for the Somme. It might be added that Haig certainly did not form a high regard for the performance of IV Corps, nor for Wilson its commander.

**Inside a British tunnel close to the entrance.**

The Germans only gained temporary relief from the attentions of the British miners for the new line was established and 176 Tunnelling Company resumed its labours by constructing a defensive lateral. By good fortune the old gallery was broken into at a depth of sixty feet and thus within days the British were back under the Germans again.

### In the Front Line

On the evening of May 19th the 1/7th (City of London) Battalion, the London Regiment took over for the first time the right sub-section of the Berthonval sector. To their left was 1/8th Lond and to their right, beyond Central Avenue, 10/Cheshires of 7 Brigade. The trenches were taken over at 9 pm - hardly giving enough light to get a grasp of the local situation; in any case, the

Motorway

Approximate area of German attack on May2

Approximate line of Central Avenue

position was confused by the indeterminate nature of the line, with the trenches already in a far from happy condition because of punishing German trench mortar fire. Two groups were sent forward to occupy advanced posts, and the rest scattered as effectively as possible. The front was hardly wired at all, overhead telephone wires had become entangled in the men on their way up to the line and routine trench work in recent days had been severely disrupted by shell fire and the looming threat of mine explosions.

The great German bombardment that opened up on the afternoon of May 21st caused terrible damage. The platoon in the left forward advanced post was all but wiped out, only four survivors managed to make it back to the British line. The right of the battalion front was completely demolished, whilst those holding White Hart Lane, two hundred yards or so to the south of the Crosbie Craters, came under most severe shell fire. Within forty minutes of the German barrage coming down telephone communications to the rear and to the left company had broken down, and the communication trench, International Avenue, became impossible to use. The Germans followed their barrage at 8 pm and were able to take possession of the British front with little resistance, the survivors being dazed and effectively left weaponless as rifles and bombs had been buried or destroyed in the relentless shelling.

The support company came out of their position in a quarry in the

Canadian Cemetery No.2

Vimy Memorial

Givenchy Road Cemetery

side of the valley and took up a position between International Trench and Central Avenue along a ridge above the Duck's Walk. An attempted counter-attack failed, and the Germans set about forming blocks in International Trench, whilst the British established a bombers' block in Central Avenue. By 9.20 pm 6/Lond had come up in support and brought in men to cover International Trench and the left flank. An attempt to move back up Central Avenue was defeated by German machine gun fire. By 10 pm the enemy artillery fire had died down and the lull was taken as an opportunity to secure positions and replenish ammunition and bomb supplies.

The problems of communication were clearly illustrated by the request for support for a counter attack by the neighbouring 7 Brigade. This was due to commence at 1 am - the request arrived at 12.40 am and needless to say 7/Lond felt unable to assist an attack which went ahead in any case. Using the ridge above the Duck's Walk as a secure line, trenches were dug almost three hundred yards forward of it and two other lines also were dug out. Consequently by the time the 'Shiny Seventh' came out of the line on the evening of May 22nd they left a tenable and deep trench system.

One of their number, Sgt F Redway, wrote of his experiences on the day:

'I am comparatively safe after the most awful onslaught the British have had in the war. We relieved a regular battalion [2nd Royal Irish Rifles] and had three companies in the line with A as a reserve in a quarry.

'Casualties occurred during the first twenty four hours; the enemy evidently got wind of our artillery being changed, for they acted at this very period. In the afternoon started the most awful bombardment of the war; the air simply rained 5.9's. It was the work of a genius. They put up a barrier of shells across the valley, preventing supplies and reserves coming up; every trench of importance was marked, observation posts etc, and our batteries were badly punished. The gas affected our eyes and I ordered the boys to put their gas helmets on, fix bayonets and prepare for anything. Upon the instruction of Lt AR Wallis I had to examine a trench, find the position of the enemy and report back to him. With a bomber for company we crawled eighty yards and upon turning a corner we rushed into two of them. One was promptly put out of action, and as we only had to report the presence of the enemy, we ran back like hell. Words fail to describe the hours up to when we were relieved, and then came a six mile march back, absolutely done to the wide. This morning we had a roll call. It was awful.'

7/Lond certainly had matters tough, but 15/Lond, the Prince of Wales' Own Civil Service Rifles certainly faced considerable difficulties in the role that they were fated to play in the battle. The battalion was summoned to move up to Villers au Bois from its billets in the woods of Camblain l'Abbe at tea time on May 21st. There was a halt near the church in Villers au Bois, and it was only when they moved eastwards from the village that they realised the enormity of the pasting that was taking place on such a small part of the ridge. Gradually 15/Lond made its way up to the support lines - by 10.15 pm the leading company (B) had arrived at Cabaret Rouge, just over two hours after the Germans had launched their infantry attack. The War Diary noted:

'We had little or no information as to what was happening, and as darkness had now gathered and we were in entirely strange trenches, there did not seem much chance of finding out.'

Captain Farquhar, commanding B Company was instructed to make contact with the CO of the battalion holding the left sub section. Almost three hours later, despite the murderous barrage in Zouave Valley, he and most of his men staggered into their destination, clutching numerous bombs and a hundred extra rounds of ammunition per man. No sooner had he arrived than he was instructed to launch an attack at 2 am - some half an hour later. It was not possible for him to be given any information about the situation and there was no time for a reconnaissance. Details were given to him of the various support troops that he would have with him in the attack - but no information as to where they were to be found. One of his flanks was to be on Ersatz Trench. The Regimental Historian finds it difficult to hide his contempt when recounting these proceedings:

See Map page 43

'.....but as he had never heard of Ersatz Trench, nor was there anyone there to show him where it was, he might just as well have been told to rest his flanks on the Unter den Linden. He was unable to find out whether there were any British troops between him and the Bosche, or how much of the line he was supposed to capture.

'However, with these scant particulars, and with the information that the objective was about 600 yards up the side of the Ridge, Captain Farquhar was ordered to start his counter attack at 2 am.'

He and Lt B Scott led their men into the attack and were both killed. Like all the other officer fatalities on this day mentioned above, their names are to be found on the Arras Memorial to the Missing.

61

'Reports differ considerably as to what exactly happened afterwards, for it must be remembered that the operations were carried out in total darkness, save for the fitful glare of the German rockets and Verey lights, and as it is difficult to get a reliable description of any battle, even in daylight, it is even more difficult to describe this scramble in the dark, in country which was strange to the attacking forces, few, if any, of whom knew where to look for friends or foes. But there is no doubt that the attack was launched at 2 am, and that B Company advanced in two waves up the slopes of Vimy Ridge, with no artillery, machine guns or Lewis guns supporting them, and that very soon they came under such a murderous and intense fire from the enemy artillery, trench mortars, machine guns and rifles, that very few survived unwounded. ...The vast majority of B Company having been killed or wounded, the foremost of the unwounded survivors, finding they were now in a hopeless position, appear to have decided to take cover in shell holes and await developments. Here they remained throughout the whole of the following day in scorching sunshine, looking for the best way of escape, and at nightfall they were able to make their way back.'

The rest of the battalion was rather better utilised and managed to make a new line along the old British reserve trench between Granby Street and Ersatz Trench. On the evening of May 22nd it came out of the line, reeling from the shock of losing most of B Company. To lose Capt Farquhar was bad enough. He was described as the best Company Commander the battalion ever possessed - keen, unselfish and energetic, he was a real pattern for all who served under him. But the loss of an individual was an inevitable part of war. What shook the battalion much more was the loss of so many of the 'originals', and a dawning realisation that the band of brothers who had come together to fight the war could be so easily ripped apart - in this case by an attack of monumental stupidity that lasted only a few minutes.

The lessons learned from this attack were numerous. The Germans had shown that a well prepared limited offensive, supported with a great preponderance of artillery, could be successful. The British suffered some 2,450 casualties to the Germans 1350. The British had learned that haphazard counter attacks without adequate preparation were a recipe for disaster, especially with wholly inadequate artillery support. Once more the problems of inadequate - or in this case any - communications had shown itself. The British still had much to learn about war.

The northern end of the Vimy sector now moved into a period of relative tranquillity - events on the Somme and at Verdun ensured that. Brigadier AC Johnston, in a letter after the war to the Official Historian, Brigadier Edmonds, described the German attack of May 21st as the best executed trench raid carried out on the Western Front.

## Bibliography

*Official History, France and Belgium 1916.* Volume 1. Brig Gen JE Edmonds.

*The History of the 47th (London) Division 1914 - 1919.* Ed AH Maude. Amalgamated Press 1922.

*History of the 7th (City of London) Battalion The London Regiment.* Comp. CD Planck. Old Comrades' Association. n.d.

*The History of the Prince of Wales' Own Civil Service Rifles.* Anon. Wyman & Sons 1921.

*Tunnellers* Capt WG Grieve and B Newman. Herbert Jenkins Ltd. 1936. Reprinted Naval and Military Press 1995.

# Chapter Four

## THE BRIGADE MAJOR'S DIARY. APRIL - MAY 1916

This very long diary extract may seem to be somewhat out of place in a Battlefield Guide, yet the period it covers is one of considerable activity on a very small part of the front. For the most part the ground described is clearly visible to the visitor in the area between the preserved trenches at Vimy Ridge and the roundabout near the Canadian Memorial to the Missing. It is a fascinating document.

The diary has been transcribed as written with some changes made in the grammar where necessary for clarity. Editorial notes are found within [], and editorial comments are in these brackets in italics.

Alexander Johnston was Brigade Major for 7 Brigade (25th Division) for much of 1916. He was commissioned into the Worcestershire Regiment in 1903 and spent several years prior to the war (1907 - 1910) serving with the West African Frontier Force. A brave man, in the course of the war he collected a DSO and Bar and an MC. He had a meteoric rise through the ranks as he noted in his diary on the day of his appointment as a brigade commander (September 17th 1917), 'I have had wonderful luck indeed to run from subaltern to brigadier general in under three years.' He was quite severely wounded within two days of taking over his new Brigade (126) and took no further part in the war. On recovery he transferred to the Army Education Corps as a Major. Retiring in 1937 as a Colonel, his last appointment was as Commandant of the Army School of Education in India.

He kept a diary throughout his Western Front service, hitherto unpublished. During the events of April and May he was in the thick of the fighting, in particular in the area around Broadmarsh crater, close to the left boundary of his brigade (indeed divisional) front. The diary extracts commence on April 21st, the day after 7 Brigade took over the line.

---

**April 21st**. Very busy day doing various things round the trenches and generally settling in. Quiet day but rain began about midday and it has rained steadily ever since.

**April 22nd**. Still raining hard with the result that the trenches are in an awful state. The Gen[eral] and I waded round the right sector: the conditions are wretched, water knee deep everywhere and very few dug-outs for the men to shelter in. [*Brigadier-General Charles Gosling*

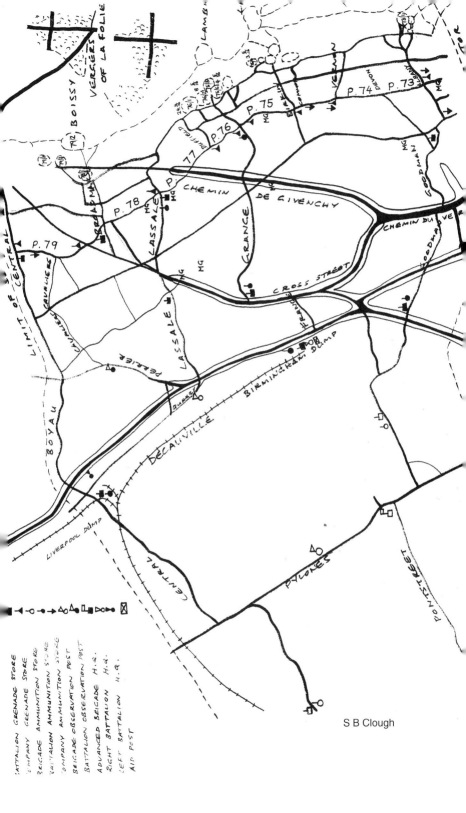

S B Clough

*commanded 3/KRRC at the outbreak of war and was wounded at St Eloi (Ypres Salient) in February 1915. In May 1915 he returned to France until wounded on May 1st 1916 (see diary entry below). He returned to command 10 Infantry Brigade in December 1916 but was killed by a shell, during the Battle of Arras, on April 12 1917. He is buried at Hervin Farm Cemetery, St Laurent Blangy, on the outskirts of Arras.*] Got back about 3 pm but had to go out again and wade through a very muddy disused trench, once a German one, to start a party at work on it at the far end. Was out again at 10 pm and had a wretched three hours - so dark that one could not see one's hand in front of one's face, standing up to one's knees in slush, rain streaming down one's neck, the darkness made useful work almost impossible, the sludge pump would not work, and the stink soon told us that we were digging up dead Germans: eventually wet through and very fed up we gave up the unequal contest! When I did get back to my dug-out I was woken up about 5 or 6 times during the night.

**April 23rd**. Another long prowl around the trenches with the Gen. Fine day and the trenches are beginning to dry up already unlike the eternal mud of Flanders, thank goodness. Our position has great possibilities if the weather will only give us a fair chance of getting to work on the trenches where we should soon have two or three lines of good trenches instead of a solitary line to try and hold on to as in the early days. Some excitement this evening as the French Mining Officer came in to say that the Germans are about to blow up a bit of the P74 Trench; also we got a secret note to say that our Intelligence believe the Huns to be contemplating a minor offensive on our front, so we are all standing by ready for some fun.

**April 24th**. In the trenches with the Gen. most of the morning and early afternoon, and very busy with all sorts of things when we got back. At 7.30 pm the earth shook like an earthquake, the dug-outs quivered, and of course we knew that a mine had gone up. We thought it must be the one near Common, which we know the Germans have got ready to send up and which our miners have told us to expect to go up at any moment. As a matter of fact it was a complete surprise to us and nowhere near where suspected mining had been heard. It was on 10/Cheshires front and had hoisted a part of the outpost line of Trench 76: beyond blowing up about 8 men it did not do so very much damage. Directly it went up both sides started an artillery barrage, and the Germans made a slight attempt to attack but were caught by our machine guns at once. 10/Cheshires got out all right with bombing parties out in front who as a matter of fact wasted a lot of bombs with wild throwing: however the digging party got out and began digging a

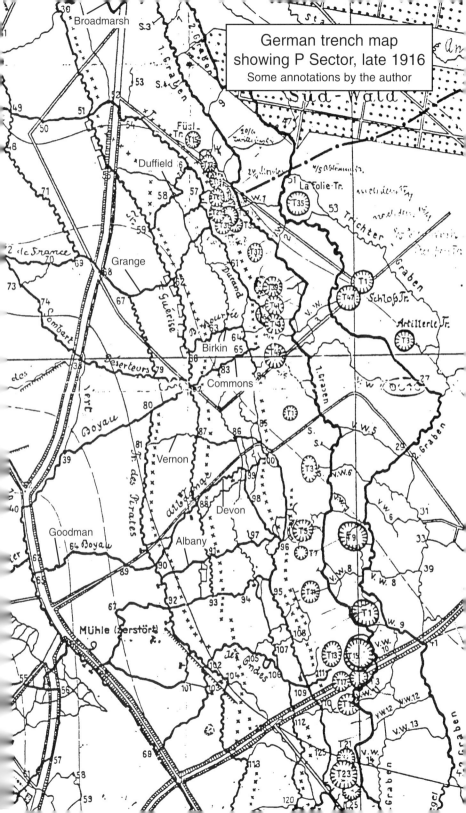

German trench map
showing P Sector, late 1916
Some annotations by the author

trench, being the near lip of the crater. In conjunction with this, and very soon after the mine went up, the Huns started a bomb attack against 1/Wilts from the Grange Crater. 1/Wilts stopped that all right but had two officers wounded and another killed in trying to go across and get in touch with 10/Cheshires. Not being quite satisfied that all was well with the latter, I decided to go up and see what the situation was for myself. Got up to 1/Wilts and went out to their Grange Crater post, where everything was all right though the Bosche was chucking a few bombs over. Then worked my way round to 10/Cheshires and found them just behind the new crater. They had begun to dig a trench and were getting on fairly well though they seemed a bit short of tools, but no attempt had been made to make a sap and form a small post at the top which could look into the crater. In fact the so called covering party were lying only half way up the slope. I crawled up therefore and had a look over the top, saw a couple of Huns calmly sitting down inside the crater who chucked a couple of bombs at me and who of course ought never have been allowed to get there; however they were soon shifted. This company (A) of 10/Cheshires, considering they were novices, had not done badly on the whole though. Having told them to send back for some more tools, to push on with the work as fast as they could, and above all things to push up a sap to the lip of the crater and form a listening post there, I worked my way back via a working party on the right to Bde HQ getting back about 2 am.

**April 25th.** Had a long day round the trenches with the Gen., and afterwards a lot to do in the office and on the telephone. About midday the Huns blew up another mine about 50 yards in front of our extreme left. Their object being not to blow any of our trenches up but to form a crater on the top of which they could form a sniper's or machine gun post. We were at an observing post when it went up, and within quarter of an hour we saw about 30 Bosches working like ants and bringing up loophole plates etc. However we got the guns turned on and gave them a bad time. This crater enables them to snipe down *Centrale* [Central Avenue] a bit but nothing out of the usual. Apparently some mining officer went back to the Division with a most alarmist report which filtered back to the Corps, and suddenly we found ourselves bombarded with questions as to the situation, what steps were we proposing to take etc etc, which we couldn't understand. However we appeased them in time though the Gen. and I had to trek across to see the Brigadier of the 74th Inf Brigade on our left, and as our so called guide lost his way we had an unnecessarily long walk. An extraordinary place, the *Talus des Zouaves*, captured in magnificent fashion by the latter last autumn, a maze of Hun trenches with hundreds of Bosche corpses in them still.

See Map
page 42

**April 26th**. Woken up at 3 am with a most awful row going on chiefly on our left. The Huns had sprung three mines and then attacked 74th Inf Bde on our left. Apparently they got into our trenches but after a stiff fight were pushed out of them all right, leaving some 30 dead behind them. Our left company got rather shelled but otherwise we were not implicated. Busy day.

**April 27th**. In the trenches all the morning. A certain amount of shelling going on and I think the Huns on this front have now got an increased allowance of ammunition. After dark went up to the trenches on the left now held by the Regiment ['the Regiment' refers to his old Regiment, the Worcesters, in this case the 3rd Battalion] and did some scouting round with Briscoe [*Capt GS Briscoe, serving with 3/Worcs*]. First visited the Duffield Crater where we have got quite a good bombing post: curious position, there is a Bosche loophole and bombing post exactly opposite on the other side, and the two watch each other like cats across the crater about 30 yards wide. From here worked our way along the observation line which is only held with bombing posts at intervals owing to the Germans having mined under most of it. Eventually got to near Broadmarsh Crater which we have never held yet but towards which a couple of bombing parties had been sent out. We carefully worked our way up an old disused trench, nearly got bombed by our own patrols who mistook us for Germans, and after going through slush and mud thigh deep got close up to the crater which we have never yet held and which 10/Cheshires had tried to take last night with two companies! Many too many men, got in each other's way, made too much noise, got a mix up in their orders and did nothing. However Briscoe and I crawled out and eventually got on to the top of the lip of the crater nearest to us, which was not occupied, though the far side was, as one could hear them talking and working. For once in a way our lip of the crater was higher than theirs, and we could really have a most excellent position. We consequently went back, got hold of a somewhat nervous corporal and a couple of men whom we made dig down a semi-made trench and form a well protected bombing post. In addition to the Huns being on the other side of the crater their trench ran along parallel to our approach to this post only 40 yards distant so one had to be careful. Had a loophole plate brought up and put into the post. Eventually got back 2 am. The Gen. very pleased at our getting a firm footing on this crater, and without any trouble.

**April 28th**. Round the trenches all morning with the Gen. and Birch [*the GSO1 of the Division, a senior staff appointment*]. At 7.30 pm again the earth was shaken to its foundations, and we knew that yet another mine had gone up. We soon heard that it was at the end of the line where the left company of the Regiment was. Apparently the 13/Cheshires on the left were pushed out of their trenches and our left was consequently completely in the air. The Regiment therefore double blocked the Centrale and started to bomb from right to left along the outpost line. It was however so wrecked by the mine explosion and the shelling that they could not have stayed there, and having bombed the Huns out they came back to a trench of ours about 30 yards behind, where they had the situation well in hand though they got rather badly shelled. The battalion on our left had gone back to their support line and by 1 am things had quietened down and the Bosche had certainly had enough of it. However, the new crater [*it was named Central Crater, after Central Avenue*] was alongside of the other at the head of *Centrale*, and the two made a sort of wall looking down his main communication trench, which would be very serious if the Huns got an MG or a sniper's post on it. The Division therefore ordered a counter attack to be made in conjunction with the 74th Inf Bde on the left: there was a lot to arrange, and the latter are a long way away so that in the

**Grenz Crater in the Albany Group blown 28/29th April, 1916. Note the two German soldiers towards the bottom of the huge hole. Immediately following an explosion each side rushed to secure the crater, or at least the lip on their side.**

end the counter attack, which could not have started before daybreak, was postponed.

**April 29th.** Very busy all day making arrangements for the attack. Had a long look at the craters from an OP, then went up into the trenches and to the head of *Centrale* and had another good look at the place to be attacked. The whole ground is just one mass of craters and shell holes, and it is almost impossible to say where anything is. Our guns, a 9.2 inch, two 8 inch, six 6 inch guns, two batteries of Hows [howitzers], two 4.7 guns and two brigades of 18 pounders began shooting steadily at 2.30 pm and then increased to rapid fire at 7.30 pm. We did not get definite orders for attack till the afternoon, there was a fearful lot to arrange, and everything was too hurried. However all the arrangements for the infantry were up to time, and the assault by half a company of the Regiment started at 8.15 pm. [*The attack was launched from Bertrand Trench, the support trench to the Front Line.*] Directly they left our trenches they were met by very heavy machine gun fire from both flanks and in front, while they got punished by artillery fire from the north; they lost heavily, but in spite of this and the roughness of the ground they managed to get close up to the lip of the crater and Parks (sic) [*Capt TG Parkes, commanding A Company. He survived the war and was to win the MC and Bar.*] and a couple of men actually got into it. They found the craters full of Germans in a consolidated position who were waiting for them and threw showers of bombs on to them. Like ourselves, the artillery had been rather rushed; they had not had time to get properly registered, and they had not damaged the enemy's position in the slightest. In fact their bombardment had been worse than useless, merely told the Germans we were coming, a whole platoon was wiped out, and the attack had failed. It was decided to make another attempt at one in the morning: there was no artillery preparation, and the men just crawled up under cover of darkness in the hopes of surprising and rushing the German trench. Again three or four of them got up to the lips of the crater, but machine gun fire opened on all sides again, in spite of our artillery making a barrage on either flank as soon as they heard the show start, and the attack had to come back from where it had started from again. Our losses for so small an operation had been pretty heavy: the enemy's shelling had been very severe - some of our front trenches being quite flattened out. [*2/Lt HA Jennings, who had taken part in the earlier attack, and had entered the crater, was killed in the second attack. He is buried at Ecoivres Military Cemetery.*] Eventually things simmered down, and all our wounded were got in by daybreak. Managed to lie down and get a rest at about 4 am.

See Map page 43

71

**Trench exit from Schleswig Holstein (Broadmarsh) Crater. The soldier is Sapper Frese.**

**April 30th**. Went round the trenches in the morning: on the left they had been pretty badly knocked about, and I think we were lucky not to have lost more than 100 men in the last two days. In the afternoon orders arrived from the Division that the Broadmarsh crater was to be attacked and occupied again, our post having been knocked off it during the fight yesterday. As the Colonel seemed to look upon it as a rather big affair and did not seem to be going about it in the best way, I was sent down by the Gen. to see him with a letter and to talk things over. It was eventually decided, I am glad to say, not to preface the show with artillery etc, but for the men to creep up in the dark with a covering party of bombers, with some trench mortars, machine guns and artillery standing by ready to fire on either flank of or beyond the flanking party if required. As a matter of fact our bombers got right on to the lip of the crater without being noticed, and as the enemy made no attempt to come over from the other lip and only threw a couple of bombs causing a couple of casualties, the digging party were able to get on digging themselves in without any difficulty. By daylight about 15 yards of good trench round the lip had been done, and a communication trench back to our lines begun: a barricade at each end gave protection from enfilade fire and, having got rations, water, bombs and a couple of machine guns up, a party of 15 men were left there for the day.

**May 1st**. Very busy arranging all sorts of working parties and doing various things including a visit to the trenches. In the afternoon as things seemed to have got pretty quiet, Gen. Gosling went back to Mont St Eloy (sic) [*Brigade Headquarters*] to get a bath. On his way back he got caught by shrapnel a long way back and got a [*shrapnel*] bullet in each leg and one in the head, while his orderly was killed - wretched luck but fortunately none of his wounds are bad, but still he will be a great loss to the Brigade. Lt Col Crosbie from 11/LF arrived late at night to take over the Brigade temporarily. For once in a way a mine did not go up in the evening so had a quiet night. [*Crosbie commanded the Brigade until May 8th; on May 10th he commanded 74 Bde, vice Brig Gen Going, until May 16th.*]

**May 2nd**. Took Col Crosbie around the trenches in the morning. Then had a busy time arranging large digging parties for the evening, and getting accommodation in tumble down dug outs for the men. Later we were warned by the miners that the Germans had got a mine to explode under one of our trenches, so we got ready for it. About 8 pm the whole place shook like an earthquake so that we thought that the mine we were expecting must have gone up. As a matter of fact it wasn't, but one just on the left; there was a lot of shelling by both sides, but nothing very much happened.

**May 3rd**. Very long and interesting day. Went out alone in the morning and was out till nearly tea time crawling all over the place. By being careful and crawling up ditches etc I was able to get to places and see things by daylight which normally one cannot do, and which gives one a much better idea of things if it can be managed. Hastily got back and rushed through some office work and arranged working parties, we were kept busy by the Huns blowing this time two mines under or near our front line: there was five seconds between them, one was under a bit of our front line and only got three of our men, and the other was about 30 yards in front of our line. The Germans were quickly out but the old 1/Wilts were quite equal to the occasion, turned a machine gun on to the Germans as they came forward, and then rushed up and started digging on the near lip covered by bombers who kept the enemy bombers back without difficulty: there was no artillery fire on either side this time. About 9 pm went out with Goddard, the Brigade Bombing Officer, to see the various digging parties along the line. [*Lt KAM Goddard, 3/Worcs, was killed in the attack on Ovillers (Somme) on July 12th. He is buried in Albert Communal Cemetery Extension.*] Also went up to both the new craters where 1/Wilts had got on in great style: there was a good deal of bombing going on, and when I had a look into one of the craters one of the Wilts bombers at my side was hit but not badly, I am glad to say. Found that our digging parties on either flank of the new craters had got on extraordinarily well in spite of a good deal of machine gun fire at intervals. Eventually got back 2 am.

**May 4th**. After setting up office work, walked back to Mont St Eloy for lunch and to have a good bath, the first for over a fortnight! Took the afternoon off, the change and rest freshened me up a lot I think. Yet another mine up in the evening, again on 1/Wilts front, and again they had the situation well in hand, and consolidated on the near lip of the crater.

**May 5th**. Round the trenches and the observation posts in the morning. In the evening went out again with Goddard, visited Broadmarsh crater and, as I had rather feared, found the state of affairs bad, no sentry on top overlooking the crater, men doing no work, and bombing posts crouching at the bottom of the trench and keeping no look out whatsoever. I am afraid that 10/Cheshires may let us down badly if we don't look out. From here went round to the working parties who were getting on well.

**May 6th**. About the quietest we've ever had, so quiet that I almost think the Bosches must be up to something. Took Birch around the trenches this morning.

**May 7th**. Had a very dull day as had to stay in and make various arrangements for this mine which we are going to let off. Spent most of the day trying to get in touch with a French officer to find out when exactly his mine would be ready, and, as I half expected, when we did get hold of him he said his mine would not be ready till tomorrow. Here we are to be relieved by the 51st Division shortly which is curious and rather interesting. I expect the shuffle is starting before big events begin. [*He was right; this was part of the thinning out process for the Somme battle.*] Went out after dinner for a short time to see the various working parties, all quiet except for an occasional burst of machine gun fire.

**May 8th**. Conference in the morning about the mine show tonight and eventually got everything fixed up. About 6 pm, in broad daylight still, of course, we heard to our great surprise that three German deserters had come in. They belonged to the 5th Guard Regiment, gave away a big relief the Germans are carrying out in front of us, and said that the Germans were going to explode a large mine at 9 pm at the head of Duffield Communication trench (the one we've been expecting to go up); as our mine was due to go up at 8.15 pm nearby, it made things interesting. The prisoners were fine looking young fellows but seemed to be very hungry and glad to be taken prisoner. At 7.10 pm we blew a camouflet into a German mine shaft near Broadmarsh CT [*communication trench*] where the Germans had been heard working, and probably some of their miners got caught. At 8 pm the Huns exploded a mine near Birkin [trench] but only buried two of our men in a post near it, and 1/Wilts were out and consolidating the near lip in no time. At 8.15 pm our own mine went up, and we turned all our trench mortars on to the German trenches just behind in the hopes that we should catch them sending up reinforcements to hold their lip of the crater. Our mine went up between the Grange and Duffield craters and, as we had expected, made it all one long crater. We had covering parties of bombers and diggers ready told off to form posts at the ends on either flank and in the centre, these all reached these posts without a hitch. The show was being done by A Company of 10/Cheshires, the only decent company that they've got. 1/Wilts managed to turn a Lewis gun onto the Germans rushing up to their side of the crater, and knocked a good many of them over. The Germans shelled pretty heavily for a bit, and there was a certain amount of bombing but they did little damage, and we were able to get firmly established on the crater. We were waiting ready for the mine to go up at which the German deserters told us about, but it never came off. Things quieted (sic) down by degrees and our casualties were very slight. We had undoubtedly blown up some Bosches and much improved our position at small  cost so that it was altogther a successful show. The new brigadier arrived during the evening, Heathcote of the Yorkshire Light Infantry. [*Charles Edinsor Heathcote was sent home on August 30th, 1916, by Major General EGT Bainbridge, (who took over command of 25 Division on June 4th) as "he was unfit for command". This caused much resentment throughout the Brigade, Johnston noting, "It is the most unjust thing I've ever heard, and the whole Brigade is simply furious. ...the Brigadier is sent home simply because he does not get on with the Divisional Commander." He was soon back, commanding a battalion, was invalided home, returned to command 7/Leicesters and in May 1917 was given a brigade once more. He retired from the army in 1932, having brigade appointments after the war.*]

See aerial photo page 81

**May 9th**. Took the Brigadier round the trenches this morning which we did very thoroughly and visited almost every part of them: the posts of the new craters seem very good. As I had expected the Division want an explanation as to why the three German deserters were able to go over to our trenches in the daylight, and eventually I had to go up to 10/Cheshires to make a detailed enquiry into the matter - obviously no proper look out could possibly have been kept, and apparently a post of 10/Cheshires, when the Germans jumped into the trench, actually bolted! At 7.45 pm the Huns blew up yet another mine, the fourth on

German fragmentation grenade from the La Targette Museum.

1/Wilts front in 3 days! It was one we were expecting, so no harm was done, and the old 1/Wilts were soon on the near lip consolidating, and had the situation well in hand at once, though there was some fairly heavy bombing for a bit. The Germans also put up a mine in front of the 74th Inf Bde on our left and the Gunners were hard at it for a long time. Also having apparently found out from the German deserters that they had got a relief on tonight and where they were going to move, our artillery fired at intervals in the hope of catching them in the middle of their relief: this was all right except that some of our howitzers dropped some short into our own trenches, but fortunately without doing any harm. We also were relieving and finished it soon after midnight without any troubles.

**May 10th.** Round the trenches with the Gen. in the morning, and again in the afternoon visiting OPs, machine gun emplacements etc. After dinner went out to see how the various working parties were getting on. Found the Regiment working hard on their trenches and then found 1/Wilts digging the P78 retrenchment where progress had been better than I had hoped for. Being very near the German trenches and a clear moonlit night, the men took jolly good care to dig themselves down as quickly as possible, particularly as there was a German machine gun sweeping our front line every 2 or 3 minutes which made one lie pretty flat! From this party I made my way across to the head of *Centrale* which had been flattened out by the *minenwerfer*, though fortunately causing us only a few casualties: here another party of 1/Wilts were helping the Regiment to repair the damage. I then went back to Broadmarsh and worked my way up to the crater. Our fellows (3/Worcesters) had done splendidly there, and one could hardly recognise it from what I had seen 3 days ago with 10/Cheshires. There were bridge traverses on the CT up to it making it much safer and easier to approach, our post was on top of the crater all right, and extraordinary good progress had been made in continuing the

76

trench behind the crater to the far edge. Just as I arrived there I had the contents of a sandbag pushed into my face! by a bullet hitting the parapet but fortunately not quite penetrating. While I was in the trench the Bosche started bombing, their first 3 or 4 bombs were short and wide, but the next came right into the trench hitting a sergeant and three men. The men under Barron however, behaved splendidly, there was no flurry or excitement though these three poor fellows were lying at the bottom of the trench. [*Capt JB Barron, Company Commander. Won the MC at Ovillers in July and a bar at Thiepval in August, where he was severely wounded.*] They just quietly sorted themselves ready for a bombing fight - "first thrower, forward" "stand by with the bombs" "straighten pins" and we all got the bombs ready to pass up to the thrower. In the meantime the men behind me at the far end of the trench quietly carried on with their digging. We did not start throwing bombs back at the Huns as we did not want to start a bombing fight if we could help it since we wanted to get on with the digging. As I thought, the Bosches having chucked a few bombs over and getting no reply thought there was nothing much doing and stopped throwing any more so that we were able to get on with our work in peace. Got the three wounded men away, none of them very bad: the sergeant with a splinter in his knee would not leave his post. If we have another quiet night we ought to get this very important trench through, and then we will be in a position to give the Bosche Hell. Eventually worked my way past another working party to Bde HQ getting there about 1 am.

**May 11th.** Had to meet the brigadier of the 152nd Inf Bde at the right of our line at 11.45 am, as he was late had a long wait in the trenches so had a good look at the Bosche trenches. Went round with Gen Ross and Booth of the Gordons, his brigade major, and showed them most of the line getting back about 3 pm. Quiet evening for once in a way and no mines.

**May 12th.** The Bosche was rather troublesome today with his shelling, putting some heavy stuff amongst other places into the Quarries and Bn HQ. As we got warning of a mine which the Huns have got ready and as a good deal of their shelling was just behind this spot, it looked rather as if they were registering their guns for putting a barrage behind the mine after they had put it up. Showed Stewart [GSO1] and Baillie of the Seaforths, both of the 51st Div Staff round the trenches in the afternoon. The expected mine did not come off in the evening after all.

**May 13th.** Wet night making these clay trenches in rather a mess. Was up in the trenches twice for various things but had an easier day than usual. The enemy put up a mine on our left a little after 7 pm, and

German trench on the west side of Broadmarsh Crater - winter 1916. This flooded section has a covering of two inch thick ice and is only passable using the fire step.

there was some pretty heavy shelling for a bit which knocked our trenches about rather.

**May 14th.** A long day out in the trenches with the Gen. Went out to all the craters and saw a lot. The Germans are shelling a good bit nowadays; no doubt the new gunners opposite us after their long rest are full of energy! and are obviously systematically registering everything. Went out again after dinner to see how our various working parties were getting on. This bit of bad weather has done a lot of harm.

**May 15th.** In the office dug-out most of the day writing out a description of the line, work proposed, enemy habits on this front etc to hand over to the 152nd Inf Bde when they come in. At 8.30 pm we blew up 3 mines on our left, and the 74th Inf Bde assaulted them and two others as well. [*The Crosbie Craters*] We got the craters all right and beat back a counter attack but am afraid we lost rather heavily though probably the enemy did also. Our line and the communication trenches were heavily shelled but not much damage done fortunately. Was up a good bit of the night sending bombs across to the next brigade.

**May 16th.** Round the trenches all the morning and early afternoon. Nice sunny day drying things up nicely. Good deal of shelling all day. Went out after dinner to see the working parties: got whizzbanged at first but no damage done, and we got on all right afterwards.

**May 17th.** Went round the trenches in the morning, a good deal of shelling all the time. When I got to the left of the line I came in for the middle of the German barrage as they attacked 2/Irish Rifles on our left. As usual the German guns were wonderfully accurate and were making very good shooting on *Centrale* CT: but somehow or other our casualties were not very heavy. The shelling went on very hard all day, and our trenches were much knocked about.

**May 18th.** Very strenuous day. Was all round the trenches in the morning and again in the afternoon showing the tasks to be done by our right working parties. As Gen Charles RE of the XVIIth Corps Staff came to stay the night to see the conditions of life in the front here, we put him into my dug out which is so small that even I cannot stand upright in it, and he is 6ft 4! [*Brig Gen JRE Charles, Royal Engineers, Brigadier General, General Staff, that is the senior staff officer for operations and intelligence to the Corps Commander, who held this appointment until mid July 1918. He then became Major General commanding 25 Division until the end of the war and ended his military career in peace time as a Lieutenant General.*] After dinner I took him out to walk him round the trenches and to see the working parties at work. It turned out to be a particularly noisy evening, a lot of bombing, and the machine guns were busy. Suddenly we heard a lot of shouting and bombing, and obviously a bombing scrap was going on. In the dark I thought it was to our left and that I heard Irishmen shouting and, as I knew they had a small show on, we went on eventually to the right of the line and then back to Bde HQ. We then heard to our disgust that 10/Cheshires had lost Broadmarsh Crater, and all the noise we had heard was the German bombers attacking and directing their fire. As 10/Cheshires had had an unsuccessful counter attack and the situation was a bit obscure, I went off at once to their HQ. Finding that their CO and 2nd in command had gone up to the trenches, I hurried on up to them as I was afraid they would be arranging a so called bombing attack, which is quite useless and merely resolves itself into both sides chucking bombs backwards and forwards and getting no "forrader". As I had feared, this was just what they had done, and it was too late to stop them. There was, as I had expected, a lot of bombing, which merely told the Germans we wanted to get the crater back, and no progress was made: in fact 10/Cheshires lost a little bit more trench. I then persuaded them to try and rush it with the bayonet, arranged for a Lewis gun to fire a magazine at 30 yards range at the enemy's block and then, before the Germans could recover, to go in with the bayonet. This plan showed more signs of succeeding and a small party got on to the Crater for a bit. It obviously upset the Germans, who put up red rockets which is their signal for artillery support, and at once they put a pretty heavy barrage on our line and behind it. After a bit they sent up a green rocket and increased their barrage with heavy shells as well so things were pretty lively. Men were coming back rather fast on all sorts of excuses, no news had been received, and as no officers were going up (only a matter of 200 yards) to find out the situation, I went up myself. Got up to the block just under the Crater and found a pretty lively grenade fight going on, but we had only a few men there and the Huns were chucking bombs down from the top of the Crater, showing themselves against the skyline at only 30 yards range. There being no officer left running the show, it had not occurred to anyone that the rifle and not the bomb was the weapon to use under the circumstances. I therefore picked up a rifle, lay up against a pile of sandbags and shot three Bosches dead right away: silhouetted against the skyline at 30 yards in the light of early dawn it was impossible to miss them. After this they kept behind the edge of the Crater and threw their bombs over without looking which made their throw inaccurate and things became easier for us. As there were so few men, I then went back to find an officer and got some men brought up. Got some men but no officer of theirs went up so went up myself again; as it was obviously impossible for us to retake the Crater I started them making a block. The Huns had started showing themselves over the top again so I got a rifle and got another fellow through the head all right. I lay there for nearly an hour while our block was being made and watched the lip of the crater; occasionally a Bosche would just poke his head up for a second, and occasionally one could see them pushing up a sandbag. I had several shots and am pretty confident that I bagged at any rate another two Bosches at least besides winging some others. Eventually with the block finished and things getting quieter I had the normal posts formed and then made my way back to Brigade HQ about 5 am.

**May 19th**. After a short sleep had a busy morning making

N

Entrance to
Grange Tunnel

Duffield

Grange

arrangements for a company of 8/Loyals [*Loyal North Lancs*] to counter attack and regain the Broadmarsh Crater. Made out the plan myself and took the officers up in the afternoon to look round: crawled out and chose quite a good place for the assaulting party to start from. The assault took place at 9.15 pm and was a great success, everything panning out exactly as I had anticipated. Twenty-five men crawled up in the dark and were told to rush the position with the bayonet, not stopping to throw bombs under any circumstances whatsoever. Close behind the assaulting party was another 25 men with packs full of bombs for use after the position had been gained, and then 50 men standing by in trenches and material ready to work and consolidate. From what I had experienced the night before I knew pretty well where the Bosches would chuck their bombs etc, so arranged for assaulting parties to go for the Crater from the west instead of from the south west. This took them by surprise, the Huns did not wait for the bayonet and the Prussian Guard left quite a lot of rifles and things behind. They then threw a lot of bombs from the other side of the Crater into exactly the area I had expected which, being avoided, caused no casualties. We knew their post and gave them plenty of bombs with the result that after quite a lively half hour our fellows were left in peace for the rest of the night to consolidate, and they made quite a good job of it.

**May 20th.** Went up to Broadmarsh Crater with the Gen. in the morning. 8/Loyals had put in a lot of good work, and the place was quite good already though the approach to it was awkward. Explained what had to be done and then worked our way along the line. Rather heavy shelling and when we got back to Bde HQ we found that was being shelled too. One crump bang into the kitchen flattened out our stove and all the kitchen but fortunately no one was there. Had several others round our dug outs, but beyond blowing some of our kit around, no harm was done.

**May 21st.** A very bad day and had my first real close experience of gas and lachrymatory [tear gas] shells. After a fairly quiet morning suddenly about 3 pm a very heavy bombardment started. The signal "Gas" was passed along, and we all got our helmets on. The shooting was very heavy indeed, and it was obvious that a German attack on a pretty large scale was impending. Our HQ, amongst other things, was shelled and wonderful accurate shooting they did too - 3 shots right into my office dug-out, several in the trench outside the mess, and the whole place got pretty well knocked about. All lines were soon cut and it was difficult to know exactly what was going on. We found out, however, that our right Bn (1/Wilts) was not affected but that our left one (10/Cheshires) was having an awful time of it which was unfortunate

**Resting from their labours, this group are constructing a dugout of sandbags during a quiet period**

as this was our weakest and least efficient [battalion]. The lachrymatory shells made one's eyes stream and gave me quite a headache. The gas shells affected some people a good deal, but of course are nothing compared to gas let out of cylinders. We got a message as late as 7.30 pm to say that our line was intact except that the left company had come back a bit and the situation with the next [battalion?] obscure. However we had already sent up a company of the Brigade Reserve. We then heard that most of 10/Cheshires officers were casualties, practically the whole of Bn HQ wiped out and that the Germans had got into the left of our support line: Oates of 10/Cheshires [a Company Commander] did some magnificent work with a few men and then came in and reported the situation to us. The Brigade of the London Division on our left had come back a long way so things looked bad. The shelling was tremendous on our left and the gas beastly, but eventually we got our left blocked and got ready to make a counter attack with 8/Loyals, our

Brigade Reserve, in the early hours of the morning. Very busy making arrangements and getting the troops for the counter attack in position. Went down to the Quarries to help Caldwell who was running the counter attack; shelling rather bad and one shell caught an awful lot of men crowded for the moment just outside 1/Wilts Bn HQ dug out. The lachrymatory gas was so bad that I could not see to write and it hurt my eyes a lot but otherwise did not affect me. Heard something from the left; the Brigade there apparently having taken the brunt of the attack and been forced to retire a good way so that our left was left rather in the air. Our detachment on Broadmarsh had held on well but had eventually been overwhelmed by an attack in really heavy numbers which they could see also sweeping down on to the 140th Inf Bde. Our counter attack started at 2 am and gained the support line without opposition, but owing to the darkness and to 8/Loyals not knowing the ground, the latter did not get any further and rather lost touch with 10/Cheshires on their right so that the situation was not quite clear. Went on myself about 4 am and found the situation was not as bad as we had thought and that really we had only been pushed off Broadmarsh Crater which was always an advanced position and out of P79. Otherwise our line was intact though fearfully knocked about and we have had a lot of casualties, but I think the Bosche lost pretty heavily too. The Brigade on our left, however, have taken a rather bad knock. They have lost all the high ground and are only just holding the eastern edge of the Zouave Valley which of course makes our left somewhat exposed.

**May 22nd**. Stayed at the Bde HQ and tried to get a rest but there was a good deal to do. The Brigade on our left was to have done a big counter attack which we were to have joined in, but it was eventually postponed. We were rather heavily shelled at intervals but it came to nothing, though it looked as if the Germans were going to attack us.

**May 23rd**. Went up to the left sector to get the exact situation and make arrangements for the evening attack. The poor old Regiment has had a bad shelling in places, and one trench was full of bodies, and 5 more men were knocked out close to me by a *minenwerfer*. In the afternoon was busy getting orders out, and went across to *Cabaret Rouge* to arrange details with the Brigade on our left who are making the big attack. From about 4.30 pm onwards there was a tremendous bombardment but I am afraid the Germans were expecting the attack, as they put down an almost impenetrable barrage, chiefly on the Zouave Valley on our left. The Regiment started their attack sharp at 8.25 pm and captured the trench all right, but as the Brigade on the left was unable to start on time owing to the enemy's artillery fire, their left was right in the air, particularly as we were a lot in front of the other Brigade at the start. Result was that they had a bad time from machine guns on their left, and in the end had to be content with holding on to the southern portion of the trench only.

**May 24th**. Went up in the early morning to see what the situation was like on our left. Met 1/60th Rifles [KRRC] who seemed a very grand lot, and found that as I expected things weren't as bad on the next brigade front as one had been led to believe. The Bosche has got what he wants eg all our mineshafts and the high ground, and has not come down the hill very much. His attack was undoubtedly an extraordinarily well run show: he systematically blotted out every trench junction and main communication trench, barraged or flattened every HQ - Bde, Bn or Coy, gassed back areas and our guns to neutralize them, and then having absolutely flattened our front trenches and dazed or killed their garrisons. They came over, the front wave men extended at about 4 paces, sending up white lights to show their artillery how far they had got, and closely followed by little columns bringing up minenwerfer and tools for consolidating. The bombing parties were closely supported by the minenwerfer, the leading bomber sending up a coloured light to show the crew of the latter how far the trench he had got. Having obtained their objectives they just sat down and prepared to meet our counter attack which they knew must come. Our left, all the same, is very much in the air and we are now busy making our communication trenches into fire trenches facing north.

---

The Division soon afterwards came out of the line; Major Johnston left Mont St Eloi on June 2nd. The Divisional Commander, Major General BJC Doran, who had taken the Division out to France in September 1915, was sacked and sent home. He became GOC Southern Command in Ireland, a not insignificant appointment, given the Easter Rebellion that had taken place in the Easter of that year. On August 28th Johnston became the Commanding Officer of 10/Cheshires.

### Bibliography
*My Diary at the War*. Manuscript record of Alexander C Johnston.

*Bloody Red Tabs*. Frank Davies and Graham Maddocks. Leo Cooper 1995.

*The Worcestershire Regiment in the Great War*. Capt H FitzM Stacke MC. GT Cheshires and Son Ltd. 1928.

*The History of the Cheshire Regiment in the Great War*. A Crookenden. WH Evans, Sons & Co. 1938.

War Diary of 3/Worcesters and 10/Cheshires.

## Chapter Five

# BROADMARSH CRATER - MAY 19th - MAY 21st

### The 8th Battalion Loyal North Lancashire Regiment win their
### Victoria Cross

The loss of Broadmarsh Crater on the night of May 18th - 19th required a counter attack by 8/Loyals to be launched on the evening of May 19th to bring the position back under British control. Edward Underhill, a twenty year old subaltern of the battalion recorded his view of the events in a letter to his parents.

'We had our blooding the night before last, as we had to retake a crater which another battalion in the brigade had lost and couldn't retake. We sent 100 men and three officers, and did it with ease. The Corps and Divisional commanders have congratulated us, and the Brigadier is very pleased.Poor little Tatam is missing, believed killed. He was in charge of thirty bombers of C Coy. Howard has a badly shattered thigh [*2/Lt Cecil Cunningham Howard, died of wounds May 25th, buried at Aubigny Communal Cemetery Extension*], and one of my best sergeants is dead [*14164 Sgt E Cocker*]. But still a price must be paid. I'm awfully sorry about Tatam; he and I were pretty good pals, and had done a lot of work together this last tour, and I'm awfully sorry he's gone. But the men were splendid, and went for it like the good chaps they are. I was up all night with Ramsay looking after bomb supplies. [*Capt Stuart Ramsay, DSO, died of wounds June 3rd 1917, buried at St Quentin Cabaret Cemetery, Ploegsteert in Belgium*] We handled something like 1,000 boxes. I have never heard such bombing as was going on then. It sounded as though there was a sort of machine gun ejecting bombs as fast as it could go. Bennett is on leave, so I am OC C Coy and very busy.' [*Lt Ernest Bennett died on August 12th 1917 and is commemorated on the Menin Gate.*]

Two days afterwards he wrote a very brief note to his mother to ensure her of his safety but that he had "been through some awful times". The attack on Broadmarsh Crater was part of a major onslaught on the brigade to the left. In the defence of the crater Lt RBB Jones fought the action which cost him his life, but won him the Victoria Cross.

By early evening the post holding the crater was cut off, from the main British positions by shell fire and gas, a bomb reserve had also been destroyed and an attack was inevitable. Lt Jones prepared his

86

**Broadmarsh Crater (*Schleswig Holstein*) firmly under German control in the summer of 1916. Craters enabled the occupants to walk about in the open unobserved.**

defences, anticipating an attack from the north (ie his left); but at 7.40 pm the Germans blew a mine some thirty yards to the south. The platoon of men holding Broadmarsh were able to keep the Germans off the lips of the new crater for some fifteen minutes. The supply of bombs for the defenders ran out, and all attempts to get more failed. Eventually Lt Jones took up a position overlooking the ground between the two craters and kept the Germans at bay with rifle fire. As he shot each of his victims he called out the number of his hits, reaching fifteen before he ran out of ammunition. Seeing some bombs nearby, he picked one up, but was shot through the head as he was about to throw it. The remainder of the defenders continued to hold out, eventually being reduced to throwing empty bomb boxes and lumps of flint. They did not finally abandon the post until 10 pm, well over two hours after the initial German assault. By this stage the battalion had been given

**Lieutenant Richard Basil Brandram Jones, VC**

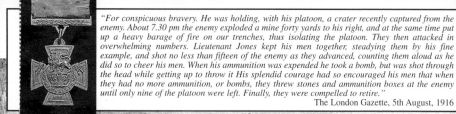

*"For conspicuous bravery. He was holding, with his platoon, a crater recently captured from the enemy. About 7.30 pm the enemy exploded a mine forty yards to his right, and at the same time put up a heavy barage of fire on our trenches, thus isolating the platoon. They then attacked in overwhelming numbers. Lieutenant Jones kept his men together, steadying them by his fine example, and shot no less than fifteen of the enemy as they advanced, counting them aloud as he did so to cheer his men. When his ammunition was expended he took a bomb, but was shot through the head while getting up to throw it His splendid courage had so encouraged his men that when they had no more ammunition, or bombs, they threw stones and ammunition boxes at the enemy until only nine of the platoon were left. Finally, they were compelled to retire."*

The London Gazette, 5th August, 1916

**An artist's impression of the action at Broadmarsh Crater where Lieutenant Jones won his VC.**

instructions to launch a counter attack at 2 am, the launch point being a communication trench between Lassalle and Central.'

The Germans withdrew with little resistance, although shell and machine gun fire had taken a heavy toll. In addition, the Germans had been extraordinarily quick in getting out wire defences, causing the battalion to be hung up on part of the line. Since the attack on the left showed no signs of making progress, the line gained was strengthened and blocks built as necessary. The commanding officer of this counter attack was Major Francis Wynne, DSO, killed in action on April 10th 1918, and commemorated on the Ploegsteert Memorial to the Missing. At 8.45 pm on May 22nd they were relieved by 3/Worcesters, but the events of the previous twenty four hours had cost 8/Loyals 126 casualties. Edward Underhill wrote a full report of these events to his parents on May 24th, though it suffered somewhat from the hand of the censor.

'They started on Sunday afternoon (May 21st) with a heavy bombardment of all sorts of shells. They gave the batteries, Mont St Eloy, the support and front line trenches showers of gas shells, which are the invention of the devil. The bombardment started about 3.30 pm. I was on the road, of which I sent you a postcard, in reserve. [This is most probably the Arras - Bethune road.] Well, about 5 pm I got orders to take my company to Cross Street, a trench about 500 yards from the front line. We got there without casualties, which wasn't bad. When we got there we walked into the gas shells and other shells, and for four hours we sat as much under cover as possible and were shelled. We only had two casualties in the company, and were very lucky. But the gas shells were beastly. One burst within five yards of me, and I was blind with tears for a bit, and nearly coughed my inside out, and my eyes were sore and ached terribly. Well, about nine, I was sent for and told that the Huns had broken through on the left. Cross Street is in our own battalion area when we're in the trenches, and the Hun had broken through on the next three battalion frontages. He had taken our outpost and retrenchment lines, which are only lightly held and not meant to be held in an attack, and also had taken our main line and support line, a depth of about 300 to 400 yards. I was told to occupy a second support line, known as Perrier, block a communication trench on my left known as Central, and hold the line at all costs, and watch my left flank. By this time there wasn't much shelling, what there was was a light barrage behind us, and it was pitch dark except for Hun flares, which were pretty continuous. Well, we dug in as best we could; the trench was battered in badly and in places there was no trench, all blown in. It was an eerie experience walking about like that, practically in the open with shell holes all round, in comparative silence after the terrific row before. About 12 we were told that the battalion would concentrate at 1 am and C Coy [ie his company] would be on the left. We were to assemble in an old disused

**Captain Edward Underhill**

trench just in front and crawl as far as possible forward, and then go for the enemy with the bayonet and drive them out of our support and main lines. Well, of course, the front was too big a one for us at our then strength. We crawled forward under rifle fire and MG fire from two guns, and heavy shrapnel, and took the support line and most of several communication trenches, but were too weak to get to the main line. I never expected to get across that 150 yards of open untouched. There

89

was one continuous stream of flares. The Huns never waited for us but ran. We found the trench very much knocked about, so set to work to dig for dear life. I got tools and bags from somewhere and we never dug so hard in our lives. It was then broad daylight and we had it quiet till 10, when the Hun started a few crumps and shrapnel and continued slowly till about 4 pm, when he set to work and we had two hours heavy shelling. We were relieved in the evening and came back to the road again, but I can tell you when I came out I was so fagged that I could hardly stand and my nerves were very rocky indeed. Everybody was pleased with what we had done on a front we had never seen before, in fact, a sort of blooming hero stunt. Then yesterday afternoon, while we were back here, the ball opened again and there was hell for several hours. And we had about four gas shells right round Coy HQ, and my eyes aren't right yet.'

Within a few days the battalion was off to the rear areas to prepare itself for its part in the Somme Battle. Lt Jones and 2/Lt Leslie Tatam are commemorated on the Arras Memorial. Jones' VC was gazetted on August 5th 1916. Edward Underhill was killed in action above Thiepval Ridge, near Goat Redoubt, on October 12th 1916 and is buried in Ovillers Military Cemetery.

**Broadmarsh Crater today begging comparison with the German photograph on page 87**

### Bibliography

*The Loyal North Lancashire Regiment*, Vol II. Col CH Wylly. RUSI, 1933.

*A Year on the Western Front. Letters of Capt ES Underhill.* Edited by his father. London Stamp Exchange Reprint, 1991.

# Chapter Six

# A BRIEF SOJOURN IN FRANCE 60th DIVISION HOLDS THE LINE

The 60th Division was formed from second line Territorial Force battalions of the London Regiment. This Division came into being in September 1914 and served at home for many months. Men from the Division were used to provide drafts for the first line battalions serving in France - for example large numbers were sent out in March 1915. Not until November 1915 did a high proportion of the infantry have .303 rifles, and the artillery pieces were even later in arriving. Serious training as a formation took place from February 1916 onwards, and the division finally went to France towards the end of June 1916.

It served until the middle of November in France, whilst in the front line in the area around Vimy Ridge after which it was sent to Salonika and took part in the Macedonian campaign before being transferred to Palestine. The division was disbanded in Egypt on May 31st 1919, having never returned to France, although some individual units were sent back in the last months of the war and replaced by Indian Army battalions.

It says something about both the relative quietness of the Vimy sector and the need for well tried divisions for the Somme battle, then about to commence, that this completely untried formation could take over such a large and vital portion of the line. The division had completed its disembarkation by June 27th and by June 29th was concentrated in the rear of its new front. It then had two weeks to prepare itself for taking over from the 51st (Highland) Division, on July 14th 1916; instructions to do so were received on July 6th.

In the short time available the Division underwent intensive training based in the fields around Penin. Trench warfare familiarisation was conducted by 51st (Highland) Division to enable a knowledge of the ground and of the enemy opposite to be passed on. Men were sent to specialist 'schools' which had been set up in previous months. These schools had become a common feature, each Army setting up a variety of such establishments, staffed by officers generally seconded from battalions at the Front. They were designed to pass on all the latest information about trench warfare, mortars, signalling and the like. Two unusual schools to which men were sent from the 60th were the Crater Consolidation School at Aubigny and the Third Army Sniping School.

The prospect facing them was not particularly alluring. As one

British officer observed, 'The observation of our front was probably unparalleled elsewhere in the British zone on the Western Front.' The trenches were still held in the same manner as when the British took over from the French.

Closest to the enemy was the Observation Line consisting of self sufficient posts, often of platoon strength, ie about thirty men. These were usually well fortified and established on the lips of mine craters or in No Man's Land. The whole front was now studded with these craters and many described it as a lunar landscape. This Outpost Line was connected by saps to the Line of Resistance, elsewhere on the front called the Firing Line, the two combined to form the Front Line. Depending on circumstances, usually to do with the ground, the Support Line lay between 100 and 150 yards to the rear of the Front, usually with fortified strong points, whilst a Reserve Line was some 400 yards or so behind this. Connecting the front to the rear were a number of communication trenches. As the enemy had such clear observation over the British lines, they wound their way over the three to four miles up to the front. This approach route was tiring and difficult. A number decided that comfort was the better part of discretion and quite a few suffered the consequences, being hit by snipers or by opportunist German shell fire. The Divisional history comments:

> 'For reliefs and heavily laden parties of men in long files continually passing along, the journey up to the line was always a very wearisome performance, especially in wet weather. Territorial Trench, in particular, which wound its way up to the line from Maroeuil, without a single cross track or means of exit till it reached the huge underground shelter of Aux Rietz, was notorious.'

The entrance to Territorial Trench was north west of Maroeuil at Brunehaut Farm the site of which is close to the junction of the D341 (Houdin road) and the D55 (the Neuville St Vaast road). On occasion it is possible to visit part of the shelter the entrance to which is near the British Cemetery at La Targette. The Regimental Historian of the Civil Service Rifles described the attributes of the Au Rietz shelter:

> 'No place on the whole British front could have been more secure from air raids and shell fire than the Aux Rietz Cave. Down wooden steps for over a hundred feet the weary infantrymen stumbled, and finally a wonderful underground world presented itself. A large cave capable of holding a thousand men, with hundreds of small candles lighting its sombre darkness, was the new home of the battalion. Down here cook

houses were established, and all were able to roam about free from bombs, shells and bullets.'

The Maison Blanche was equally capable of housing a thousand men in its vast underground cavern, though it was not so roomy as its northern neighbour. Au Rietz was also the site of an Advanced Dressing Station the Collecting Posts for this being at Neuville St Vaast and at the forward part of Territorial Trench.

The Au Rietz ADS was situated in deep dug-outs providing excellent protection from the incessant shelling, inevitable, given the importance of the position as a road junction, a communication trench junction and the presence of a light railway line. Consequently casualties could only be moved at night-time. The Main Dressing Station was in the village school at Ecoivres, and the Casualty Clearing Station was at Aubigny, handy for the railhead so that serious casualties could be easily transported to Base Hospitals in the rear, such as at Rouen and Etaples. Those whose injuries or illnesses required a

**Above: The road from Maroeuil at the La Targette/Au Rietz end.**

**Below: Plan of the Advance Dressing Station at Au Rietz. As sketched by Colonel D Rorie, RAMC.**

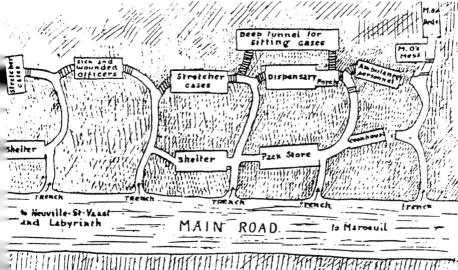

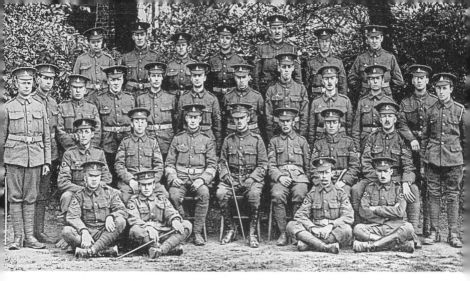

**NCOs of the 2/4th London Field Ambulance RAMC.**

respite from the trenches but no further evacuation than the divisional area were taken to the divisional Rest Centre at Hautes Avesnes, which in the three months that the division served in the sector, handled over three thousand cases.

See Map page 128 and 67

The front that the division covered ran from Central Avenue in the north to a point in the south about a thousand yards north of Roclincourt. Although mine warfare was not fought on the same scale as in earlier months, there was still plenty of activity, far more of it now initiated by the British. On July 26th the Germans blew a new mine under Duffield Crater; during the same night the British blew two new mines creating a massive crater 80 yards across from north to south and 120 yards across from east to west. Named Tidza, or sometimes Tidsa, both these craters still exist. Duffield Crater is immediately behind the visitors' centre, near the preserved trenches and it is inaccurately labelled as Du Field Crater. Tidsa is to the right of the path that leads to the German line adjacent to Grange Crater.

The firing of Tidsa provoked a furious fight, but the near lip was eventually secured by 2/20th London Regiment. Amongst other casualties two officers were killed, Lt T Gardner and 2/Lt G Hellicar, who are buried at Ecoivres. Trench raids became more common (at least by the British) although the firing of mines also continued. On August 16th a new mine was fired by the Germans under Grange and the British managed to secure the near lip, although the Germans made a spirited attempt to isolate them by coming around between Grange and Tidsa and cutting them off.

On August 11th at 12.30 am the British fired a large mine which was named Pulpit. The site of this is in the fields on the opposite side of the Neuville St Vaast - Thelus road from Zivy Crater, itself preserved as a mass grave by the War Graves Commission. It is about two hundred yards into the field directly north of Zivy, either in the lee of, or incorporated into, the motorway. The British put down a barrage on the far side of the lip, and the crater was secured after twenty minutes of fighting and four hours of consolidation by the 2/13th London Regiment (2/Kensingtons). Lt S Killingback RE was killed in the action and is buried at Maroeuil British Cemetery.

Trench raids were used by the British to determine how the Germans were reacting to events on the Somme and also to discover whether and when German formations were being moved to that battlefield. 2/Kensingtons launched their first ever raid on August 6th from their front in the area of the Pulpit Sap. This was to be a bombing raid consisting of two officers and 33 Other Ranks. Preparations were thorough; facsimile trenches were constructed at Aubigny over which the men practised for several days so all could be quite clear as to the parts they had to play. The party came up with the rations to battalion HQ, established at the Boyau des Abris. A box barrage was laid down around the German section of trench to be attacked, and the raiders set off at 10 pm. Tapes were laid out from the British front to indicate the way home, but these soon suffered from German shellfire. Two flanking parties secured the area for a bombing party to work its way along the German trench. The raid was on a fixed time limit to prevent the Germans from having the time to react in strength, and no German was found to be taken prisoner. Some members of the party got cut off by the German barrage from the trenches, and spent an uncomfortable day in a shell hole before they were able to make their way back to the British line at 1.30 am on August 8th. Several other raiders became completely lost in the dark, and in the absence of the tapes ended up going in German trenches. Their leader, 2/Lt F Stockwell was killed, and is commemorated on the Memorial to the Missing in Arras. Another soldier also got lost whilst assisting wounded men to get back, and found himself in the German trenches. Although armed with nothing more lethal than a pair of wirecutters, he grabbed a German and succeeded in making it back to the British lines together with his prisoner and the wounded men. The raid had cost ten casualties with little reward.

2/London Scottish (2/14th London Regiment) spent most of their time in the N sector, to the east of Neuville St Vaast. The support line followed generally the line of a metalled farm track 200 metres beyond the Neuville St Vaast cemetery on the left hand side. Opposite is a

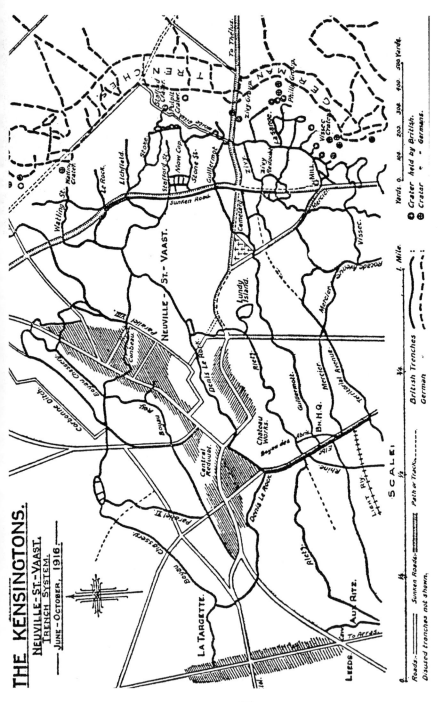

**Officers of the 2/13th London Regiment (Princess Louise's Kensington Battalion.**

recently extended metalled road. It was deep, well constructed and housed the Headquarters dug-outs of the three companies in the line spread out along its length. Features of the line were Zivy Cave, near the road junction on the cemetery side, Paris Redoubt, a semicircular trench forward of the front line, and on the right Argyll Crater, believed at that time to be the largest on the Western Front. Battalion Headquarters were in the Support Line, just beyond a fork in the Neuville - Ecurie road, where Sapper Trench came into Elbe Shelters.

The Regimental historian describes the battalion's time in the trench as follows:

'There are writers who have talked of the monotony of trench life. Few of those who have had the experience will speak of it thus. True there is little that merits notice in a history of the time, but the ceaseless vigilance, the unending work, the constant 'new stunts' of the enemy which have to be met and defeated, the days and nights of discomfort, cheerfully endured, call for a determination no whit behind that which is the key to success in the grand assault.'

The battalion launched a raid on the Germans on the night of September 29/30 directed against the German trenches at the northern end of Paris Redoubt so avoiding the line of craters that fronted this position. Undergoing training similar to that of the 2/Kensingtons, the party was slightly larger - two officers and 45 Other Ranks. The additional men provided a covering party in addition to the flanking and snatching parties that were in that raid. This covering party, equipped with a Lewis Gun and a telephone with direct contact to the covering artillery,

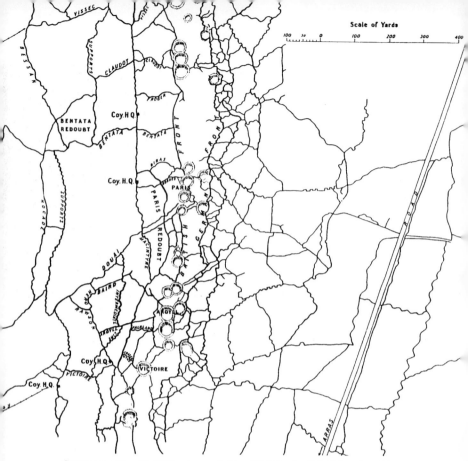

**Sector near Neuville St Vaast occupied by 179 Brigade, 60th (2/London) Division between July and October, 1916.**

was detailed to cover the right flank, vulnerable as it was because of the cover offered to the Germans by the craters. The raid was launched under the protection of a barrage at 2.15 am, the men wearing football jerseys and body shields and having blackened their faces. Opposition was encountered in front of the German line from a number of their outposts, but the line was gained and a number of prisoners sent back including an English speaking corporal and *Feldwebel*, a German Company Sergeant Major. Time was running out, but the telephone line to the artillery ensured that the barrage continued for five minutes, thereby enabling the raiders to get away with relatively light casualties, in all nine, of whom three were killed.

The 2/Civil Service Rifles (2/15th London Regiment) generally served in the line in rotation with 2/London Scottish. They too launched a raid which was rather more successful than many others, losing only one died of wounds and several wounded, whilst achieving their objective. German trench mortars continued to irritate and a particularly nasty specimen of the species, which fired a round three foot long and some twelve inches in diameter, provoked a reaction. To attack the Germans a deep emplacement was made in the Bessan Redoubt and a heavy British mortar was brought up which fired 'flying pigs'. This weapon of destruction provoked mixed feelings; the presence of the Trench Mortar Officer and his men in the front line area was rarely a cause of rejoicing amongst the British infantry.

Soldier of the 2/15th Battalion The London Regiment Prince of Wales Own Civil Service Rifles.

'To fire it [the 'flying pig'] was only an experiment so all the men in the trenches in advance of the emplacement were temporarily withdrawn lest the shell should accidentally fall short. The test was successful, and large craters about ten feet deep and twenty yards wide were made in the Hun lines. However, the experiment was not taken by the Huns in the right spirit, and retaliation on his part for the next few days was very brisk. A strafe from guns and minenwerfers of all calibres was poured on to the unoffending infantrymen's heads. Dug-outs were blown up, but the resultant casualties were small.'

Officers of the 2/15th Battalion The London Regiment Prince of Wales Own Civil Service Rifles.

Towards the end of October the division left the line, however it was only in early November that it learned that its destination was not to be the dreaded Somme but rather to Salonika. Until the Anglo-French forces were able to engage in combat against Bulgaria, and to overcome the hostility of the Greek Government, not to mention that of the Greek Royal Family (the Queen was the Kaiser's sister), they spent months in 1915 and 1916 doing very little. Indeed the Kaiser referred to the quarter of a million or so allied troops who were there as being incarcerated in his biggest Prisoner of War camp. These considerations were of no great concern to the men of the 60th Division; they were out of the maelstrom of the Western Front.

## Bibliography

*History of the 60th Division.* Col PH Dalbiac. George Allen & Unwin. n.d.

*The Kensingtons. 13th London Regimen*t. Sgts OF Bailey and HM Hollier. Regimental Old Comrades' Association 1935.

*The London Scottish in the Great War.* ed JH Lindsay. Regimental Headquarters 1926.

*The History of the Prince of Wales' Own Civil Service Rifles.* Anon. Wyman and Sons 1921.

*A Medicos Luck in the War.* Col D Rorie. Milne and Hutchison 1929.

# Chapter Seven

# TUNNELLERS UNDER VIMY RIDGE

Many who visit the Canadian Memorial Park at Vimy will take the opportunity of going underground into the Grange Subway. It is the only such system, at least on the British part of the Front, open to the public. This sometimes leads people to draw the conclusion that this was the only place where subways, or underground passageways, were used. This is not so as, for example, in the line to the south of the La Bassee canal twenty miles of subways were constructed,

'In nearly all cases there was sufficient room for men in full kit to pass along in comfort, while at intervals passing places were provided. Many of the subways connected with machine gun posts, and, for defence purposes, traverses were made into which loophole plates were built. Generally the subways were lit by electric light - in order to minimise confusion, good lighting was essential. ...There can be little doubt that the subways were a decided success. In addition to providing shelter, they were used sometimes in connection with raids. They also gave the feeling of security and reduced casualties.'    (*Tunnellers*)

Closer to Vimy, to the east and south east of Arras, tunnels were driven out from the numerous caves, tunnel and sewerage systems under the city. These were linked up, providing a vast underground barracks with ventilation, light, water and latrines where 11,000 troops were sheltered in the winter of 1916 - 1917. Subways were driven from the caves out to the front; thus my grandfather, serving with 7/Leicesters, was able to come underground from the centre of Arras to just behind the line at St Laurent Blangy. On the opening of the Battle of Arras on April 9th 1917 some British troops 'actually passed from the security of the caves direct into the German trenches', situated on either side of the Cambrai road.

As mentioned earlier in this book, mining activity peaked in June 1916 but declined particularly after September largely because of the German decision to construct a completely new defensive line, known to the British as the Hindenburg Line, some twenty miles behind their existing front. Their aim was to cut out the Noyon Salient, shorten their line and thereby save considerably on manpower required to hold the line. It was also intended as a means of spiking allied offensive plans for 1917. Certainly the withdrawal did not commence until February 1917, and whether intended or not, the new dispositions did upset the 'decisive' offensive planned by the new French Commander in Chief, Robert Nivelle.

To compensate for the loss of the disruption to the enemy caused by their mining activities, the Germans intensified their use of heavy trench mortars. The disruption caused to the communication trenches and the blowing-in of mine shafts was felt by both infantry and tunnellers. The only solution was, where the ground allowed it, to build subways to provide protection and a secure means of communication and the bringing up of supplies. The bigger subways were extended to include first aid and command posts, ammunition and other dumps, electricity generators and large water tanks, tramways (using wooden tracks and rubber wheels to deaden noise) and even small gauge railways. The system existed on a number of levels. Mining operations could also be carried out from them, but special precautions were taken for any gas that might result from detonations. The water table was highly variable and could rise considerably in winter time; whilst water also seeped through from the surface. In the Grange subway the visitor is informed that if it rains heavily on the surface, three days later it rains below. Consequently the tunnels were all constructed on a slight incline, and periodically there was a sump to drain this water away.

In the Regimental records of the Argyll and Sutherland Highlanders are notes for a lecture on mining, written by J Young, a surveyor who as a subaltern served with 185 Tunnelling Company from February 1916 until the close of mining. The following are selected extracts from these notes.

Strength of Company with attached infantry was about 1000 men during the three months [*internal evidence suggests that this relates to the period of the construction of the subways, prior to the Battle of Arras*].

**Boring tools**. None were used in mining work. All face work was done by pick, two or two and a half pound pattern. The wombat drill was used for making chimneys for dug-outs and ventilation when necessary and possible in subways.

**Explosives**. Ammonal used in mines, but only two small craters blown by us.

**Organisation of shifts and supplies**. Men worked on 3 shifts and changed over at the face. Supplies were ordered daily and reached HQ that night and material was taken up to the nearest dump following night by GS Wagon [*General Service wagon, horse drawn*], lorry or rail.

**Timber supports**. All square setts, 6" by 3", usually four feet apart in galleries and closer in entrances where steps were formed

Listening to the the sound of digging as 'Tommy' drives yet another tunnel towards their lines. Counter measures consisted of digging a small tunnel quickly and blowing what was known as a camouflet - a small charge sufficient to spoil the operation.

for the easy disposal of chalk. [*Once a tunnel had served its purpose, timbers were often removed and used elsewhere, for there was a chronic shortage of suitable timber on the Western Front. One of the advantages of the ground in this area was the ability of tunnels to be relatively stable for some time without supports; another was that the clay served to muffle the sound of mining work.*] All chalk taken in sandbags to a dump where the ground was trenched, and then earth was thrown over the chalk. *Disposal of chalk was a big problem, as it was a complete giveaway of mining activities. Placing the spoil near trenches solved this problem to a large extent as the ground was already excavated, and liable to shelling, also producing chalk.*] We did use camouflage in some places but not generally.

**Listening Posts**. All done by Geophone and Western Electric [*electronic listening devices*]. Generally two listening posts per shift at hours fixed at different times each day for 10 minutes. [*At this time all work would stop so that sounds made by the Germans could be heard*] All faces visited for listening twice per shift. Results all plotted each night at HQ when daily reports came down, and record kept continuously. The Listening [*reports*] compared favourably with survey of enemy mines which was made after the Battle of Vimy Ridge  Progress made per shift of 8 hours was at least four feet and no tunnellers were allowed to get off with less, and if ground was soft enough considerably more was expected. When mines were down to the depth decided and levels were being driven it was decided to put the wind up Fritz by a policy of wedge picking. This policy was carried out in each mine by the men using wedges and tapping them in the way that pick work would sound to the enemy. Our intention was to get Fritz to blow his mines before we got near them - not only to save our galleries but also to destroy his own and thereby indicate his position. The infantry headquarters were informed that the sap head areas were now dangerous and must be held very lightly.  Unfortunately they would not take our advice.

On April 28th 1916 Fritz blew 11 mines between 10 and 11 pm on L and M sectors [*the area to the east of Roclincourt*] and did great damage as the forward saps were strongly held. The only mines blown by us were fired to get rid of two advanced galleries which were too exposed to keep and were only in clay and sand. [*In fact his memory has played him false. The Germans fired 13 mines at 1.30 am on April 28th. The blast caused numerous casualties and severely damaged trenches and dug-outs. One Highlander was found the following morning buried up to his shoulders, but still alive. The Germans had tried to dig him out and take him prisoner, but had to withdraw. Before doing so they swiped him over the head with a shovel, to no permanent ill effect. This explosion caused severe resentment amongst the infantry against the tunnellers, as they felt let down by them. The tunnellers took consolation and professional pride that the blasts were exactly where they were predicted to be by the listening posts.*]

After the enemy blows of April 1916 we pursued our policy of protecting the front line and had no damage done to our galleries by any subsequent blows made by Fritz.  In N sector there was a

"strip to which 6"×3" legs were wedged.
Roof was close lagged with 8"×1"×4½ ft.
white wood. or other timber & sides were
lagged when necessary.
Shaker cut was as follows.

Wood rails?
Rubber tyre bogies

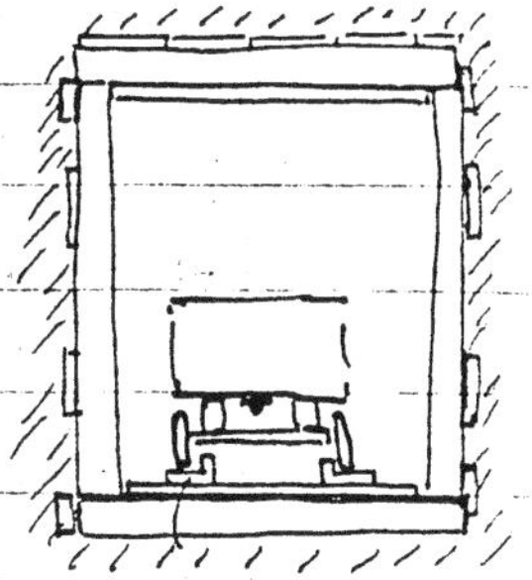

Sand. & Clay.

15-20 ft. L+M. 2-10 ft N Sector

Broken Clay. Chalk with Flints

15-30 ft.

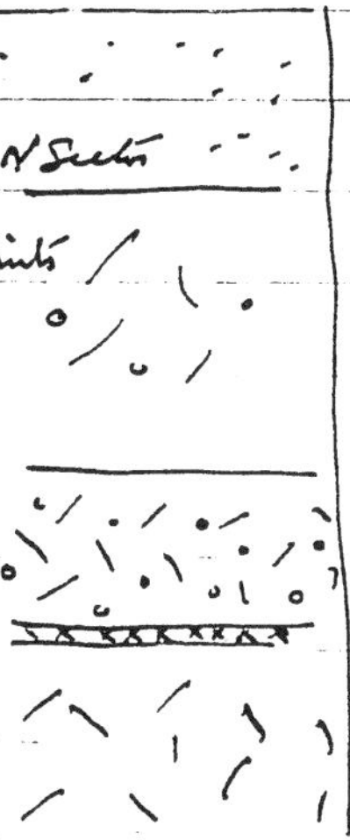

Ventilation from Winch
Chamber by Holman Air
Pump & 3 (?) Tubes.
when necessary

Hard Chalk. with Flints.

20 ft.

Sandstone. 15"

Hard Chalk.

water bearing.

water level varied at
least 15 feet & was at
maximum in February '17
in L27 Gallery.

Survey of German mines gave water level rising to 215 to
216 in various galleries ... in Nº 112 There was 6 ft of
water in shaft when surveyed in May 1917. & Gallery
was submerged at Shaft Bottom.

**Extract from notes on mining by J. Young.**

105

good deal of mine fighting [*So much so that Byng, the Corps Commander, became seriously concerned and changed the Tunnelling Company on the Neuville St Vaast sector*].

See Map page 131 and 157

(When we took over) there was then less activity in the enemy galleries and listening reports gave only intermittent activity at a few points. The day for mining warfare was over and the men so employed probably more urgently required elsewhere. At the close of 1916 preparations were being made for the Battle of Vimy Ridge. Tunnelling Companies were asked to drive subways for the safe passage of troops from the reserve to the front line and No Man's Land.

**Notes on Mining Procedure on the Labyrinth Front**. When L and M sectors were taken over from the French very little mining had been done and the enemy appeared from our listening posts in various galleries to be in a strong position. All French galleries were in advanced sap heads and we decided to start afresh from the front line which was held by the 51st Division. The principle adopted was to get down quickly to a depth of sixty to eighty feet below the surface and then push straight ahead and simultaneously branch left and right to cover the front as quickly as possible. Two entrances were driven down (in clay) to a winch chamber which had 15 foot cover (minimum). From this chamber a dip mine was driven at 1 in 5 or 1 in 4 to the depth decided on. The entrances were all timbered to finished size 6′ x 4′ inside timber and winch chambers would be 6 foot high and about 15ft by 9ft. Dip mines were 4 or 5ft x 4ft inside timbers and the illegible [?levels?] 4ft x 4ft. The roof was close lagged with 8″x 1″ x 4′6″ white wood or other timber and sides were lagged when necessary.

**Barricade Subway** was driven under the crest of a hill about half a mile behind the front line and gave a safe passage to troops coming from the rear past a road crossing which was always subject to heavy artillery fire. Total length including entrances 1300ft. Dimensions were 6ft x 6ft inside timbers. Cover 30 feet.

**Douai Subway**. A subway system parallel to a main communication trench with several entrances from it. The forward exits gave access to forward trench as jumping off point into No Man's Land. Accommodation constructed for Brigade and Battalion HQ, Dressing Station and Signals. A Petters Oil driven generator installed for Electric lighting throughout. Accommodation for troops was found by connecting to M36.

**Bentata Subway**. [*Called Bertata on map of subways*]. This

106

German sappers in the trenches at Arras. Standing is Sapper Piefke in front of Tunnel 23 (see page 116). His working dress is made of drill, the cap from a sandbag.

**Winter conditions in Schleswig Holstein crater.**

system covered ground that was under direct enemy fire and in principle was the same as Douai Subway. Chambers each had entrances and exits.

**Zivy Subway.** This connected up to a chalk mine working and was also connected up to our mining system and gave advanced jumping off points for the troops on April 9th. All galleries were completed before the end of March 1917.

Total lengths (entrances, exits and galleries) were as follows: Barricade 1300', No 1 Section; Douai 2370', No 2 Section; Bentata 2680', No 3 Section; Zivy 2680', No 4 Section. Total 9030'. [Almost one and three quarter miles or three kilometres]. ....the work was done in three months.

Outstanding Events. The craze for record driving in 24 hours went on for some time and eventually 185 Coy did 62 feet, 6' x 4' timbered and lagged four feet apart in 24 hours in a subway for the Canadian Corps in 1917. All material was trolleyed from the face in broken chalk. There were six men per shift of six hours, two men at the face, two trolleying and two resting for twenty minute spells. No 4 Section did this on three occasions under different sector officers. I think it varied from 60 - 63 feet on each occasion and 62 feet was accepted as far as I remember.'

To the north of 185 was 172 Tunnelling Company. They drove three subways, Grange (over 800 yards long), Goodman (1,880 yards) and Lichfield (about 500 yards). The first two had a series of heavy trench mortar emplacements and secure storage for ammunition. They also laid three mines - yet another one under Broadmarsh and two smaller ones near the end of Grange. In the event the Broadmarsh crater mine was not fired. The infantry often did not like mines being fired as part of an attack as it made the crossing of No Man's Land difficult and unpredictable. In any case the situation had been complicated by the Germans firing nine mines shortly before the attack, creating the Longfellow Crater which may still be seen in the Memorial Park.

182 Tunnelling Company constructed the four subways in the Berthonval sector: Cavalier, Tottenham, Vincent and Blue Bull. As the ridge was steeper here these were all generally shorter than the ones further south. The exits for all these subways were in Zouave Valley. Vincent connected with the mining system whose main gallery was enlarged and pushed forward to surface in No Man's Land. 176 Tunnelling Company had the Souchez Sector where mining was still active at two levels, 60 and 110 feet. There were two relatively short subways, Coburg and Gobron, some three hundred yards long, and these were about fifty feet below the surface. This Company also laid three mines, one of which was placed under Kennedy Crater. The reason for placing new mines under craters was because the Germans had converted them into strongpoints and they offered the possibility of disrupting any attack with flanking fire. The Grange Subway is more fully described in the touring chapter of this book.

These subways were complex pieces of construction. Dangers from gas both natural and from explosion necessitated the placing of gas curtains and doors. Ventilation for latrines, generators and kitchens was provided by earth augur bore holes to the surface. An earth augur was a drill that could bore small diameter holes (say four to eight inches) many feet. The Dressing stations had operating tables and signal cables ran into the mining system and along the laterals, which ran the whole length of the front at this point. Generators were petrol driven and the fuel stored in fireproof dug-outs, as was the ammunition. The electrical arrangements were the responsibility of the specialist Australian

Electrical and Mechanical Mining and Boring Company; this unit was used in all the subways. To make sure that people did not get lost brightly lit signs and direction boards were provided. Even today in the relatively small section of the Grange subway open to the public there would be plenty of scope for confusion without a guide.

The work of the tunnellers had developed beyond recognition from their humble beginnings in 1915. By winning the mining battle and by the construction of the subways they played an invaluable part in the victorious attack on Vimy Ridge.

It is of some interest to note how the German miners operated. These are the edited comments of Lt Olaf Grieben who was serving with 9 Res. Pi. Bde. 19.

There were three troops in a mining company which alternated in the mine with each other. One troop was 'in position' for twenty four hours, departure from accommodation was at 6 pm and mining operations would last from 8 pm to 8 pm the following day and would then return to billets. However the engineering officer in charge had to remain in position for three days. His task was to maintain contact with the CO of the infantry battalion of the sector and to supervise the mining and the listening. Most of the time he was on the surface. The trenches deteriorated more and more and it was very hard even to walk. Difficult decisions had to be made especially when, according to listening reports, British blow ups were to be expected and the infantry had to withdraw from their trenches within the danger zone. There was always the risk that the British would realise the situation and take possession of those empty trenches without a fight.

The decision to give such advice was quite a responsibility for someone who was just over 18, as Lt Grieben was.

## Bibliography

*Tunnellers* Capt WG Grieve and B Newman. Herbert Jenkins Ltd. 1936. Reprinted Naval and Military Press 1995.

*War Underground* A. Barrie. Frederick Muller Ltd. 1962.

*Battlefields of the World War* DW Johnson. New York, OUP. 1921.

*Geological Influence on tunnelling under the Western Front at Vimy Ridge* MS Rosenbaum. Proceedings of the Geological Association 100(10, 135 - 140.

Notes for lecture on mining activities in the Vimy Sector  J Young. Held at Argyll and Sutherland Highlanders Regimental Museum.

# Chapter Eight

## CANADA ON VIMY RIDGE

'The whole Canadian contingent, unsurpassed in potential quality, had made rapid progress in efficiency during the winter months, and by the spring of 1917 it had been welded into a fighting force as well qualified for its great task as any formation on the Western Front.' (*Official History, 1917*, Vol 1.)

This summarises the vital contribution made by Canadian troops in World War I. Of all the great battles in which they participated, none compares in emotional importance to the people of Canada than Vimy Ridge, part of the Battle of Arras, which commenced on April 9th 1917. There is a large body of readily available literature on the attack on Vimy (see bibliography at end of book) and this section aims to give only the briefest outline, concentrating rather more on individuals and units. The Canadians arrived on the Souchez sector of the Front towards the end of October 1916, exhausted from their labours on the Somme around Courcelette and beyond, although the 4th Division did not move north until the very end of November. (There were four Canadian Divisions, described as 1st, 2nd etc Canadian Division. For

**Reinforcements marching through the outskirts of Arras, 1917.**

the sake of brevity I shall drop 'Canadian' in this chapter.) At the beginning of March they were positioned on the Vimy Front, with 1st Division in the south, just north of Ecurie, working in numerical order northwards to the 4th Division, whose northern boundary was below the Pimple. By late November Byng, their British Corps commander, had been briefed by General Sir Henry Horne, commanding First Army, concerning the allied offensive plans for 1917. The task of the Canadian Corps and of I Corps to its left was to win the Vimy heights, thereby securing the flank of the Third Army, under General Allenby, for its attack to the east and south of Arras.

General Currie.

Byng now set about training his men for the task that lay before them with his mind on this major attack to take place soon after mid March. The key to the winning of the battle would be the volume and weight of his artillery and the effective manner in which it would be used. This will be discussed later in this chapter. Developments would also be required in infantry tactics. Byng sent Currie, one of his divisional commanders, to join a group of senior British officers to Verdun to find out what lessons had been learned by the French as a consequence of the battle there that had raged there for ten months in 1916, more especially in the successful counter offensive of December. The result of this visit, and of consultations taken throughout the Corps, was the conclusion that advancing in waves was no longer suitable (if it ever had been). There was now a greater possibility of flexibility with a more experienced artillery; and many of the NCOs and junior officers had gained considerably more experience in fighting over the months that they had been in France. This meant that small groups would be allowed greater initiative; objectives would be a natural feature and not just a line of trenches that had in all probability been obliterated. Full use would be made of developments in communications and all precautions taken to ensure their maintainance.

A policy of raiding the enemy trenches was followed with rigour keeping the Germans perpetually alert and wary. The raids often caused considerable casualties to the defenders and severe damage to their trenches and dug-outs as well as building up the experience of junior commanders and knowledge of the front that faced them. They were frequently extremely successful but on occasion went very wrong. The Canadians suffered considerable casualties as a consequence of these raids, many carried out at company and even battalion strength.

Such a large raid took place on the night February 28th - March 1st. No less than four battalions of the 4th Division were to take part, providing a total of 1,700 troops, launching an attack on the high point of the ridge, Hill 145 (where the Memorial now stands) and where the German defences were particularly strong. To cause maximum disruption amongst the enemy the intention was to use gas prior to the infantry assault.

The lack of a favourable wind had caused the attack to be delayed for two nights, which would have had its effect on the keyed up troops waiting to get on with a raid for which they had spent so much time in preparation. Eventually the conditions were right , but by the time the tear gas was released at 3 am the wind had changed direction once more towards the west. The Germans were alerted and opened up with their

**British soldiers on the Arras front taking up duckboards under the cover of night.**

artillery (both high explosive and gas) and small arms, and to illuminate the scene. The forming up of men for the attack was disrupted, those in exposed positions outside of the trenches becoming helpless victims of the heavy German bombardment. Nevertheless, at 5.40 am the attack took place against a thoroughly alert enemy. Hardly anywhere did the attackers make any sort of impression on the German line; indeed the German front line positions were only lightly held, so that when the Canadians did break through, in considerable disorder as they were, the large concentrations of Germans in the support lines ejected them with ease. By 6.25 am the survivors, having fought their way out, were back in their lines.

The 72nd Battalion (The Seaforth Highlanders of Canada) were in the right centre of the raid. This battalion had had one highly successful raid on February 16th against the German lines opposite Ersatz crater. All the raiding party of 56 returned safely after causing considerable damage to the Germans, not least by the use of a heavy charge of 60 pounds of ammonal that was hurled down a dug-out. The Battalion faced the new challenge with enthusiasm.

See Map page 43 and 157

The men for the raid were deployed in the front line, in Granby Avenue (a communication trench) and in Vincent Tunnel (alongside Vincent Street). The Germans put down a barrage on the Front Line only ten minutes or so before the attack was scheduled to start. A Company, attacking from the Canadian front line trenches, gained their objective with little difficulty. D Company, on the left and operating from Granby Avenue, were able to make their objective and grab ten prisoners, but were forced to halt any further exploitation by well directed machine gun fire. The men of B and C Company, operating from Vincent Tunnel, were victims of their own gas. Things were made difficult by the Germans concentrating their fire on the entrance and vicinity of Vincent Tunnel. Only half of B Company had made its way over the top when further disaster struck in the shape of the Canadian's own gas. German shell fire broke open some of the gas canisters in the trench and this led to complete confusion. Thus half of B Company and all of C Company were forced to abandon their attack.

Whilst A Company held the German front line, D and B Company pushed forward, faced by,

'a sea of mudholes of all sizes and depths, everywhere linked together and filled with water. A passageway between them would be attempted only to prove impracticable, and it would be necessary to return and make a new attempt to find a road forward.'

Eventually objectives were reached, demolition charges fired and some prisoners captured. However the captors became the captives when they lost direction and were surrounded by the enemy. The withdrawal was relatively orderly, but already A Company was busy with the business of collecting some of the many wounded. At noon on March 3rd a most unusual sequel to this raid took place.

'...two German officers carrying a white flag were seen to leave their front line and stop in the middle of No Man's Land to the right of the Battalions front. An officer of the 87th Battalion which was holding the line at this point went out and met them. They expressed their intention to carry our dead half way across No Man's Land in order that we might bury them in our own ground. An informal armistice [was agreed] all along the front concerned in the raid of March 1st and on the 11th Brigade front to the right where the heaviest losses occurred; many bodies were brought across in this way.'

Of all the raiding battalions the 72nd had been the most successful and suffered the fewest casualties. The Canadians had suffered 687 casualties, including two battalion commanders: Lt Col Kemball of the 54th and Lt Col Beckett of the 75th who were both killed. They, along with many others killed on this raid, are buried at Villers Station Cemetery. They had captured just 37 prisoners.

A more successful raid on January 27th 1917 almost resulted in the

Miserable conditions for British and Germans alike on the Arras front in the winter of 1916/17. Dugout entrance of a German engineer officer.

death of Lt Grieben. That day was the Kaiser's birthday, with special rations and spirits were very high. In addition his unit was on the move from Vimy Ridge – on January 30th it was despatched to the rather more peaceful surroundings of the Swiss frontier. He was sitting in Tunnel 23 discussing Listening Reports. [*Tunnel 23 was opposite the northern part of the Chord, probably somewhere in the north eastern part of Canadian Cemetery No 2, in ground captured from the British on May 21st 1916.*] He described what happened,

'The noise of the battle increased more and more, with the sound of artillery and English heavy trench mortar bombs. Suddenly a voice shouted from the tunnel entrance:

116

Sapper Dohl struggles to make the rounds of the tunnel system in front of The Chord (a part of the British line).

German trench map dated 25 November, 1916. 1:3600. The German galleries opposite the Canadian Lines clearly illustrated.

Inset: Leutnant Grieben struggles round his command.

"Herr Leutnant der Tommy ist in Graben!" I stepped back when I heard someone or something tumbling coming down with a noise. It wasn't the caller but an English shaped charge which tumbled down with a lot of noise and step by step. The charge, probably with a delay detonator finally came to rest immediately in front of the minehouse. Everybody in our dug-out was terrified. If this charge had exploded all our lives would have been lost. But nothing happened: it was a dud. "All men out of the dug-out through the entrance!" No shots were fired. Outside the caller was lying prostrate; a British club had bashed in his skull.'

Preparations for a large offensive require tremendous efforts to build up the infrastructure to support the attacking infantry and artillery. Huge dumps were required for the vast array of artillery being marshalled. On top of this were great quantities of other stores, food and fodder that would be required to maintain the greatly increased number of troops that were gathering on the Vimy sector. 28 miles of roads had to be repaired and then maintained. Eleven trainloads of building materials and gravel were brought in every day. Three miles of wooden plank road were constructed and specialist forestry troops were used to provide wood from the local forests Railway troops were brought in to maintain and expand the rail and tram network. The arrival of 50,000 horses (mainly to provide the motive power for all the wagons moving the supplies) required a

Behind the lines on the Arras front, British pioneers lay a light railway track.

dramatic improvement in the water supply - new reservoirs were built, bore holes driven, 45 miles of pipeline laid and pumping stations installed producing the 600,000 gallons that the Corps required every day. 21 miles of signalling cable were buried seven feet deep to protect them against all but the heaviest shells; 66 miles were laid above ground. In addition there was the great engineer effort by the Tunnellers described previously creating the underground refuge of the subways.

The artillery concentration of the firepower of seven divisions, and eighteen independent artillery brigades, was of far greater density than had been available on the first day of the Somme. On top of this were

**Preparing to lay down a heavy barrage prior to the Canadian assault on Vimy Ridge. The earlier failure of the French to take the ridge had been blamed on inadequate artillery fire - Byng was not going to make the same mistake.**

the big guns of eleven heavy artillery groups and the artillery of I Corps on the Canadian's left. This force provided Byng with 377 heavy guns, over 550 eighteen-pounders and over 150 4.5-inch howitzers. At Vimy there was a heavy gun for every twenty yards of the 7,000 yard front and a field gun for every ten yards. On the Somme there had been a heavy gun to every sixty yards and a field gun to every twenty yards. The allocation for the operation was 42,500 tons of shells with a daily quota of 2465 tons. The French had blamed their failures to take Vimy Ridge in the attacks of May/June and September to inadequate artillery. Joffre wrote in June 1915, 'It is essential to concentrate on the front to be assaulted sufficient artillery, heavy and field, to crush all resistance.' Foch wrote in October 1915 that failure was due to 'the lack of a sufficiently accurate or an adequate artillery preparation. None but our heavy batteries could demolish the formidable frontages that confronted us.' This does not detract from the fact that the French put down an enormous artillery barrage, especially for the assault of September 25th, but still did not capture the ridge.

Byng wanted to ensure that the artillery achieved all of which it was capable. He procured as many of the recently introduced No 106 wire cutting fuses as possible; this fuse exploded a shell as soon as it made contact with the earth or the wire. This was an essential part of the plan to destroy the German wire, which had hitherto depended on shrapnel bullets to perform the task, with indifferent effect. He instructed his Gunnery commanders to ensure that a high level of performance was

# VIMY, 1917.

## The Concentration of the Heavy and Siege Artillery
### for the attack of the Canadian Corps.

Map 9.

XXXI

BULLY
GRENAY

6

Double
Crassier

XV

AIX NOULETTE

LENS

I.

LXXIX

Bois de
Noulette

24

LIÉVIN

AVION SWITCH

LXXXIV

Bois
de
Bouvigny

+ N.D. de Lorette

Bois en
Hache

Bois de
Givenchy

Bois "Triangle"

AVION

XXVI

Bois
de
la
Haie

ABLAIN
ST. NAZAIRE

CARENCY

SOUCHEZ

The Pimple

GIVENCHY

LA CHAUDIÈRE

VILLERS
AU BOIS

II CDN.

Cabaret
Rouge

HILL
145

4 Cdn.

Bois de
la
Folie

PETIT
VIMY

VIMY

CDN.

XXX

Bois des
Alleux

LXXVI
LIII

B. de
Berthonval

Berthonval
Farm

3 Cdn.

LA
TARGETTE

Aux
Rietz

NEUVILLE St.
VAAST

2 Cdn.

LES
TILLEULS

Bois du
Goulot

Count's
Wood

HILL
135

Hornet's
Wood

Station
Wood

FARBUS

Bois de
la
Ville

Théouanne

THÉLUS

Farbus
Wood

MONT St. ELOY

I CDN.

1 Cdn.

Nine Elms

ECOIVRES

L

Bois de
Maroeuil

Brunehaut
Farm

LXX

FOND DE VASE

ECURIE

ROCLINCOURT

51

XIII

MARŒUIL

St. Pol

Scarpe R.

Gy R.

LXIV

St. AUBIN

XLIV

XVII.

34

9

Scarpe R.

ECURIE

XVIII

ARRAS

15

VI.

## REFERENCE.

| HEAVY | SIEGE |
|---|---|
| 2, 60-pdrs.; or 2, 4.7" Guns. | 2, 6" Guns. |
| | 2, 6" Hows. |
| | 2, 8", or 2, 9.2" Hows. |

XVIII — XVIII Heavy Artillery Group

Note. The positions of the batteries were the ones
originally selected

Compiled in the Historical Section (Military Branch).
Ordnance Survey 1939.

SCALE.

Yards 1000  500   0        1000      2000       3000       4000      5000       6000       7000      8000       9000      10000 Yards achieved, and that all scientific methods should be used to ensure both accuracy and speed. He expected his guns to be able to fire effectively against unseen targets and to be able to shoot closely over the heads of the advancing infantry. A command organisation had to be established that could manage to best use all this abundance of artillery. The use of the rolling barrage, the establishment of silent batteries (ie ones that did not fire until the battle commenced, thereby concealing their presence), the registration of guns on their targets and development of skills in counter battery work were all items of major importance.

The biggest enemy of the infantry was the artillery. Therefore it was imperative that as much as possible of the enemy artillery should be destroyed before the infantry became exposed. The Royal Flying Corps and observation balloons were the most important elements in spotting enemy artillery and observing the fire put down on their battery positions. A more recent development was to take bearings on their gun flashes. Lt Col AG Haig, the Field Marshal's cousin, was working on a system of sound location, based on microphones placed in different positions which recorded the sound of firing and explosion of the shell. The Canadians developed this further with the use of the oscillograph. The result of this was not only the location of German batteries but an increasing knowledge of how the enemy was likely to react and use their artillery in a particular set of circumstances.

All of this preparation, the vastly increased British interest in the German positions on the ridge shown by numerous raids and RFC flights, the bustle of activity behind the line and the presence of more and more artillery units must have been obvious to the Germans. In fact

**An innovation, armoured cars in the streets of Arras - they would be used in the event of a breakthrough.**

The infamous 'General Winter' made life miserable for all but especially for the thousands of horses and mules engaged in moving loads behind the lines.

Byng was unconcerned about this and made no secret of the fact that an offensive was in the offing - just the time and the date were unknown. The Germans made no effort to interfere, a quite extraordinary situation for which the German Court of Inquiry established after the battle could find no satisfactory explanation. In fact it was felt that the Germans were planning a withdrawal from the Ridge - nothing else could explain their inactivity.

The biggest problem felt by the Canadians came from General Winter - the ground became a quagmire in the changing weather conditions and the roads suffered tremendously under the strain of traffic. The poor horses and mules suffered great hardship, many of them dying in their traces, and it was a losing battle trying to get them buried.

The artillery bombardment on the First Army front began on March 20th and in this first phase of thirteen days only about half the batteries were brought into action. From April 2nd onwards the rest of the artillery joined in just as Third Army, to the south, began its massive programme, concentrating on the German villages just behind the Canadian lines, such as Farbus, Thelus and the two Vimys. The front line trench systems were the responsibility of heavy mortars, the smaller varieties being used to deal with the wire. Machine guns firing indirectly were used to harass the enemy behind the lines, targeting communication trenches, road interchanges and the like, in the hope of catching ration and working parties or the movement of trench supplies.

Thus by the time the attack was launched on April 9th, thirty times the amount of heavy artillery ammunition had been used than in the French attack two years previously and more than double, proportionately, to the quantity of all types that were used in the Battle of the Somme before July 1st.

Gunner Frank Ferguson served for much of the war in the 1st Canadian Siege Battery. His battery was positioned in the suburbs of Arras, in St Catherine, to the north west of the city. His diary gives some idea of what life was like for the gunners.

**22nd March**. Fritz still pounding Arras with big stuff. When they are coming over it sounds as though all the trains in the world were rushing through the air at the same time. Tonight no less than 600 rounds of ammunition were brought up in the lorries and dumped right in the road for us to wash and get ready for the big push. Six hundred 9.2 shells are a lot of shells in anyone's language, but judging by the tones of this bunch of mulligan hounds who must wash and pile them up, profane is the only tongue that can adequately describe their opinion of them.

**30th March**. The battery fired 200 rounds at trenches near the Three [*probably meant to be Nine*] Elms.

**3rd April**. The outfit got orders to be ready at noon to send over ten minutes of 'rapid' - meaning load them up and fire as fast as possible for that length of time. Boy, we had no sooner got started than one of his planes camped right over our position, and before that well known phrase 'Jack Robinson' could be uttered by a man who stutters, they had all the ammunition factories in Germany falling on us out of the clouds. What a strafe that was; no less than three times we had to take to the big dug-outs. The position looked as though someone had dug it up with a big spade, and the shells which the boys had piled up so nice and neat were thrown all over the scenery, a lot of them cracked and unfit to use in the guns.

**7th April**. Again in the evening he strafed us right royally with the result that he smashed in five of the boys' dug-outs. ....We had to run through an alley between two walls, so with head up yours truly spurted for the field across the road and places where the German shells were strangers. Bang. The first thing I knew I was on my back on the ground. Unhurt, but annoyed and surprised, I got up and started to run again only to find myself on my back again. This happened several times before I became aware that I was caught up in a telephone wire dislodged by the shelling. North was laughing to beat the band, but it was some time before I could see the humour of it.

**8th April**. Easter Sunday.  During the night 1420 shells arrived on lorries  and all hands are busy washing them and putting them in nice neat rows.  Had to roll them for a while.  Then went to the guns to fire 500 rounds.  A swell lot of Christians we are.

**9th April**. Was awakened this morning before daylight by a terrific bombardment.  What a sight in the dim light as the guns put down the barrage for the boys to go over and try for Vimy Ridge.  What a terrible racket as all the guns on the front blended into one continuous roar and the flashes from them made the effect of a great electrical storm

Private Donald Fraser had been a member of the 31st Battalion serving in France for a year when he transferred to the 6th Brigade Machine Gun Company on September 22nd 1916.

**February 23**. We are in a deep dug-out [*beside Ecurie*] constructed by the French out of chalk and capable of holding thirty six men.  There are two entrances at the ends which create a strong rush of air through the interior making the place on the cold side and very draughty.  Two tiers of wire bunks run from end to end.

**February 25**. Tonight I shot away a couple of thousand rounds of indirect fire. Indirect firing is not very satisfactory - you cannot see your target and, of course, do not know what damage, if any, is done.  Besides, the belts have to be refilled and it is a blistery job forcing the shells in with the palm of the hand without a protective covering.  [*The Machine Gun Companies used the belt fed Vickers Machine Gun as opposed to the lighter Lewis gun used by battalions.*]

**February 28**.  I am cook today, and this is the menu.

Breakfast:  Rolled oats, bacon, bread dipped in bacon fat.  Tea. Dinner:  A mulligan made from meat, crushed hardtack [*a hard army biscuit, not unlike a dog biscuit*], rolled oats and oxo cubes, seasoned with salt and mustard.  Supper:  Bully Beef fried with bits of bread.  Bread with plum jam and lemon marmalade, cafe-au-lait. The rolled oats, oxo cubes and cafe-au-lait were either purchased privately or obtained from parcels received from relatives or friends.  We have been feeding pretty good since the last few days. We are doing quite a lot of indirect fire on dumps, communications, etc.

**March 27**.  Tonight a number of us were detailed to carry rifle ammunition from a dump beside a road leading out from the north side of Neuville St Vaast to a point several hundred yards

125

further up Vimy Ridge. As the roads and terrain were in a sodden, muddy condition, we were directed to a spot in a trench where several pairs of long rubber boots lay and were told that we better make use of them when packing up the boxes of shells. We looked them over carefully and found that they were for most partially filled with mud and water and decided against their use. However a few hardy souls struggled into them. We started together on the job, but it was not very long before we separated and got strung out. Up and down the trail we went, sliding and slipping and emitting curses in the darkness until we found that Moodie, one of the rubber boot fanatics, was in dire distress. Then our misery turned to levity......he was determined that he would not discard them. Wearily he struggled on. ...We had carried 144,000 rounds. It was a fatigue that we will not readily forget.

The Canadian objectives were divided amongst the divisions of the Corps as follows: 4th Division, Hill 145 and later, on April 12th, the Pimple; 3rd Division, the strongly held position of La Folie Farm; 2nd Division, Thelus - and because its front broadened as it broke through the German lines, was assisted by 13 Brigade from the British 5th Division; 1st Division, Hill 140 and working in conjunction with the 51st (Highland) Division on its right. The attack went extremely well with the exception of the 4th Division on the north of the line, where the German defences around Hill 145 held matters up until they were overcome on the afternoon of April 10th. In addition to a first class barrage (though one element of surprise which was maintained was the lack of an intense barrage just before the attack went in, and so offering no sort of warning to the Germans) the Canadians had the

**Heartbreaking for the French to see some of their finest buildings such as this one in Arras slowly destroyed under the enemy's barrages.**

advantage of a bitter north westerly wind at their backs, complete with snow and sleet. This lengthened the darkness of the night and severely obstructed German observation of the attack, limiting the effectiveness of their remaining artillery.

The Canadians suffered over 7,700 casualties in the two days of fighting, of which just under three thousand were fatal.There were 3,400 German prisoners taken up to midnight of April 9-10. The whole of the main part of Vimy Ridge for a length of 7,000 yards and a maximum depth of 4000 yards had been captured. It had been an outstanding feat of arms, a success which was in large measure shared by the British divisions in the Third Army operating to the south. The battle continued after April 9th, but lies outside the scope of this particular guide.

The day is examined from the viewpoints of participating units working from the south northwards.

## THE FIGHTING TENTH

The 'Fighting Tenth' (Tenth Battalion Canadian Infantry) was part of the 1st Division (commanded by Currie), 2nd Brigade. For the attack it was on the left of the Brigade front. Its first objective (on the Black Line) was the *Zwolfer Stellung*, the last of a series of trenches that marked the German forward zone. Just beyond the crest of the ridge was the second objective (part of the Red Line), the *Zwischen Stellung*, which as its name suggests was the German Intermediate Line. The battle had been planned on a leap frog principle, with lines (Black, Red, Blue and Brown) indicating progress and where new battalions might be required to take over the next bound depending on the individual divisional plan.

See Map page 128 and 178

For military supplies the battalion was allocated 75,000 rounds of small arms ammunition (saa), 200 Mills bombs (ie grenades), 500 rifle grenades, hundreds of Verey lights, ground flares and SOS rockets. Furthermore they had considerable engineering supplies, including picks, corrugated sheets and barbed wire.

The 500 yard front through which the 10th had to attack was dominated by Victoire Crater and the Argyll Group, of which Nos 1,2 and 3 were across their front. Advancing across them would be difficult, not made easier by muddy conditions, in turn made worse by the incessant churning which was a consequence of the shelling of the previous weeks. There was about one hundred and thirty yards of passable front and the Germans had wired the ground between the craters which would naturally be covered by machine gun fire. An officer's patrol went out on the night of April 4-5 and came to the

See Map page 98

127

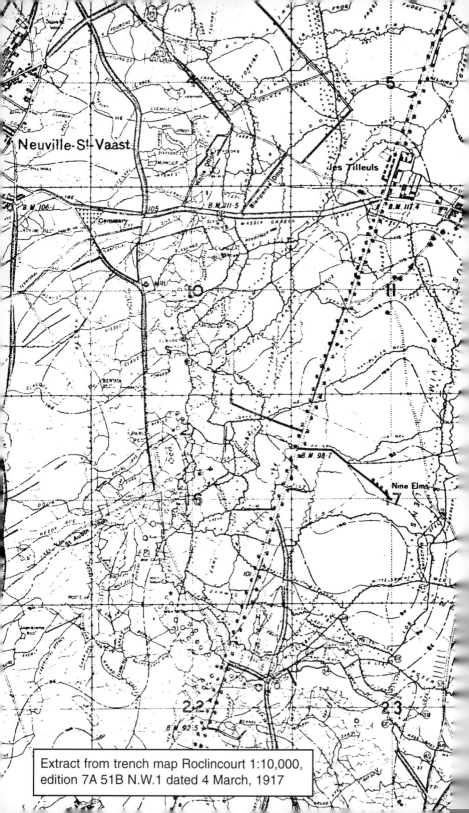

Extract from trench map Roclincourt 1:10,000,
edition 7A 51B N.W.1 dated 4 March, 1917

conclusion that the ground between Argyll 1 and Victoire - about sixty yards - was sound enough. Between Argyll 1 and 2 there was only four yards, and the ground much pocked by shell fire, Argyll 2 and 3 were actually touching and thus formed a block. Sending soldiers across the craters was not a realistic option as the walls of the craters were so steep and unstable as to make progress difficult, and in any case it could not be certain what awaited them in the crater.

A raid on Easter Sunday showed that the artillery had not seriously damaged the foremost

Constructing ladders to assist the attacking infantrymen leave their trenches during the forthcoming assault.

German defences; Currie instructed the Tenth to move back from their forward positions and then put as much artillery fire as possible on the German line which had the desired effect. The situation for observation had been made much more difficult for the Tenth because of the obstruction of the enemy lines by the craters; the Germans had gained dominance (with Richthofen's Circus) of the air and so observing was not possible by this means.

The attack commenced all along the front at 5.30 am. It is interesting to note that the men were carrying approximately the same weight as were the men on the First Day of the Somme, for which the generals have been much criticized. The infantry needed to take with them the means to hold and fortify their new positions and have the ammunition and supplies to hold out against immediate counter attacks. It would be impracticable to expect any effective form of resupply during the first hours - even day or so - of a major attack for a number of reasons, ranging from enemy artillery fire to the difficulty of movement over ground that had been heavily fought over.

The Tenth experienced most of its casualties in the first minutes of the attack, with the enemy bringing down effective small arms fire. The artillery had removed the chief obstacle, the wire, and within fifteen minutes or so Toff Weg, the German resistance line, had been captured. The battalion moved across the Arras - Lens road and their Black Line objective, the Zwolfer Stellung. The loss of officers might have proved serious, but all ranks had been taken over replicas of the

129

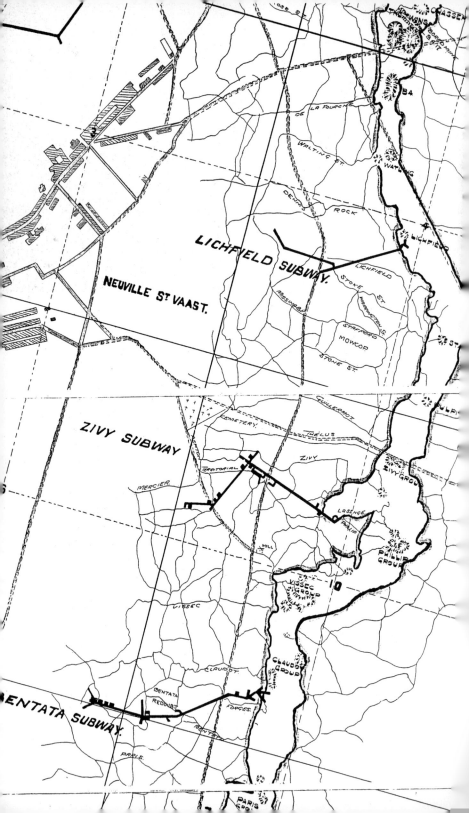

An attack on the German lines underway.

battlefield and knew their tasks - accordingly NCOs were able to fill the gaps effectively. The Black Line objective was taken by 6.10 am, although the Germans were now pounding the battlefield with gas shells - shells which they had been stockpiling for a planned premptive attack on the Canadians on the north of Vimy Ridge. The Battalion now had half an hour in which to reorganise, reallocate manpower in order to make good some of the losses and keep the balance of the assault, and appoint new commanders (usually NCOs) to replace fallen officers. So it was that a CSM (Company Sergeant Major) led B Company at 6.45 am into the next phase of the attack on the Red Line position of the *Zwischen Stellung*. This was captured by 7.10 am with relative ease.

The task of consolidating the line was made that much easier because the German artillery was far from sure where the Canadians had now got to; and in any case their batteries had suffered so much from the counter-battery fire of the previous days. In due course the assault was taken on by battalions from 1 Brigade. The Tenth had gone into the attack with just over 760 men; on April 9th it lost 374, of whom over 100 were killed. Even the best laid plans and the best conducted operations have a high price when set against such an outstandingly capable foe as the Germans.

### THE SIXTEENTH (CANADIAN SCOTTISH) CEF

The 16th Battalion (Canadian Scottish) Canadian Expeditionary Force were also in 1st Division, but in the Brigade to the north of the Tenth. They too had carried out rehearsals in the marked out fields around Servins; tapes and multicoloured flags indicating enemy dug-outs, trenches, roads, machine gun emplacements and artillery positions. A relief map in plasticine showing all the contours of the Ridge was on view at First Army HQ, where parties of officers and NCOs were brought back to study it. Preparations completed they started up for the front at 6 pm on the Easter Sunday.

'The evening, in marked contrast to the days which had gone before, was calm and sunny with a light wind blowing from the west, which was fast drying up the ground. Marching up the valley between the Ecoivres and Maroeuil woods, they passed by the battalions of 1st Brigade - the 'passing through' brigade - which was scattered along the sides of the hollow with bands playing, waiting for dusk to permit them to move on. They reached the high ground, under distant view of the Ridge from where the German was making his last survey of the wide land he had dominated for two long years before, and halted. After the bustle of the previous days there was a strange quiet; all vehicular traffic for that night had been cleared off the forward roads; the sound of the gunfire was carried away from them over the enemy's country by the breeze.'

The 16th made its final approach to the front by using the Bentata Tunnel, and therefore sustained few casualties. However Battalion HQ suffered a disaster when it transferred to its Battle Headquarters because the Commanding Officer, Lt Col CW Peck, decided not to use the subway as it was out of the way and crowded with men and so the HQ went overland. An officer commented,

'Going forward the mud was terrible. In one place I had to get out of my boots, climb on the bank of the sunken road and then pull out my boots after me.'

A shell landed on the group of six men, and the only one to come out unharmed was the CO. The adjutant was dangerously wounded and See Map page 98 blown up into the air by the force of the explosion. This calamity was the most eventful part of the assembly. The Sixteenth faced a similar problem to the Tenth as regards the state of No Man's Land, in this case craters in the Claudot and Vissec groups causing the problems. The initial advance was made in files of sections, these coming under fire from machine gun posts placed on the further lips of the craters and heavy casualties, especially amongst the leaders, were suffered.

'The fire from the hostile machine guns now beat in on the advancing men from front and flank alternately. It was evident that these weapons were scattered everywhere in an irregular pattern on the shell-pitted ground over which the Battalion had to go forward. Men began to drop singly, others in huddled groups. The action could best be described as a running fight, men rushing from shell hole to shell hole, the bodies of the fallen indicating by their position the location of the enemy's guns towards which this fighting was directed. Organised enemy resistance was first met with at a trench called *Visener Graben*, thirty to forty feet yards short of the Arras - Lens road; this trench had somehow escaped destruction by the supporting artillery. In it the Germans fought hard and the trench had to be captured at the point of a bayonet.'

Private W J Milne

The battalion was to win its second VC of the war here. The left hand company was held up in its progress from *Visener Graben* to the *Zwolfer Weg* by machine gun fire from its left threatening to cause a serious delay to the advance and attempts to silence it failed. Private WJ Milne sprang out of a shell hole and crawled forward on his hands and knees. When he reached the gun position he killed the crew with bombs and captured the gun. He dealt with a similar situation on the advance to the Red Line and was equally successful. However he was killed later in the day and so his VC was posthumously awarded. His body was never found and he is commemorated on the Vimy Memorial. The battalion took its objectives on the Red Line on time. The men looked behind them as fresh troops came to continue the battle.

'But of more intimate concern to 16th men was another group which had just arrived from the rear. It was headed by Pipe-Major Groat and Piper Al McNab, playing lustily. Then came Colonel Peck, next RSM Kay followed by the Colonel's servant, and last of all Kay's batman with a jar of rum under each arm. At first the company men were too occupied with the consolidation work on hand to show their feelings. The scattered cheer was heard, but as the procession drew nearer and got into the final objective, a volume of cheering broke out on all sides, apparently directed in greater part to the last figure with the jars.'

As the battle progressed into the afternoon and men went forward to the far side of Farbus, it was possible to realise fully the meaning of the victory of that morning.

'A wide expanse of open country - green fields, woods and villages untouched by war - stretched to the skyline for miles on all sides. On the easterly horizon the smoking factory chimneys of Douai were plainly visible and some men announced that through glasses they were able to observe the clock dial on a high tower. ....A fugitive horseman, apparently pursued by bullets, was zig-zagging across the plain, clinging with hands and knees to the neck and body of his steed; enemy guns were standing on the open plain of Willerval, deserted by their crews.'

The Battalion suffered 341 casualties on April 9th; 454 by the time it came back to the reserve on May 4th. This included 25 officers - of the 21 who went into action on April 9th no less than twenty were put out of action - 'the heaviest officer casualty list for any single action of the war'. Amongst their number was Col Peck, who had to be evacuated to England, but was able to return in due course to his beloved battalion and who went on to win the Victoria Cross in September 1918 at Cagnicourt.

## THE 13th BATTALION
## (ROYAL HIGHLANDERS OF CANADA) CEF

See Map
page 130

The task of this battalion on April 9th was to follow the 14th and 16th Battalions and provide support should they have difficulty in attaining their objectives, and to consolidate the ground won. The battalion was 'disappointed' not to be in the forefront of the attack, but their role as support to the attack was not insignificant. The 13th also had use of the Bentata Subway.

'The Bentata Subway runs from Claudot Avenue to the front line, between Roger and Claudot Trenches. This will be used as a covered route during bombardments previous to zero hour and after zero hour for runners. At the top and bottom of each entrance are notice boards showing to whom the entrance is allotted, and where each entrance or exit leads to.'

Once the German positions were captured duties became mundane but specific.

'Escorts for prisoners will be provided in the proportion of 15% [ie 15 escorts to every 100 prisoners]. Escorts should, as far as possible, consist of slightly wounded men. Prisoners and escort will march overland and not by communication trenches. .....Salvage: All arms and equipment found in the area between the *Eisner Kreuz Weg* and Old German Front Line will be dumped at the junction of Claudot and Bentata with old British Front Line. The 13th Battalion is responsible for the burial of all dead between *Eisner Kreuz Weg* and the old British Front Line. Lt JL Atkinson is detailed to supervise the clearing of the Battlefield in the above area. He will work in conjunction with and under the supervision of the Divisional Burial Officer. [*These men were buried in Nine Elms Cemetery*]

The Battalion suffered relatively few casualties, following on behind the 14th Battalion. By early afternoon on April 9th the carrying parties had brought forward to the dumps on the Arras - Lens all that they had been assigned. Battalion HQ was established in *Neuberger Haus*, a large German dug-out.

'Here the Herr Commandant had just celebrated his birthday, the walls being festooned with wreaths of evergreen, while enshrined amongst them there was an ornate sign, *'Zum Geburstag.'* Soda water bottles were much in evidence, but the only food that the curious Highlanders could discover consisted of some very filthy looking sausages and a large quantity of *'kriegsbrot'*, which resembled sawdust and was utterly unpalatable.'

The 13th Battalion gained rather more than it expected as a consequence of Vimy Ridge. The 73rd Battalion, also Royal Highlanders of Canada, was disbanded. This battalion had been part of the difficult Fourth Division attack, forming the left hand flank battalion of the Corps. Because this Regiment had three battalions at the front, and its source of enlistment from Montreal was not sufficient to maintain them, the youngest was lost and it members split amongst the other two, the 13th and the 42nd. The 13th gained the 73rd Pipe Band - this combined with their own produced a band of fifty, compared with the official establishment of six.

## THE ROYAL CANADIAN REGIMENT

This Regiment was part of 7 Brigade 3rd Division on April 9th. An unusual feature of its composition was that earlier in the year it had received a large draft from the 97th Battalion, also known as the American Legion. This unit had a majority of United States citizens in its ranks, so that the RCR became quite Americanised; the vast majority of them remained with the battalion even after the United States entered the war in April 1917. The 3rd Division only had two lines to gain, Black and Red, and a distance of about 1200 yards to cover to the Final Objective. The battalion carried out its rehearsals for the attack on marked out fields near Houdain. On April 7th it moved up from Villers au Bois and made use of the Grange subway, using the section between the Grange and Wedd Street entrances for protection and accommodation prior to the assault. In the early hours of April 9th the 648 men moved out to their jumping off position along the Observation Line running from the north of Birkin Crater to the northern edge of Vernon Crater. When all the objectives had been gained a party of 50 men were to establish a Strong Point (No. 5) which was to be

See Map on page 137 + 139

135

**Sweet success! The Ridge is firmly in the hands of the Canadians. Some are seen here regrouping in a German communication trench.**

garrisoned by them and two heavy machine guns from the Machine Gun Corps. This was designed to secure the newly won ground from German counter attack. In addition two smaller strong points were to be established on the Final Objective.

The initial attack went smoothly - 'a few dazed Germans were captured in the craters that marked the first obstacle in the unit's path' - rather as the rehearsal had envisaged. The artillery had done its work here most effectively and the enemy trench system ceased to exist in many places, and killed many Germans. The first 700 yards to the Black Line objectives went smoothly and were covered in the allocated thirty five minutes. The final objective, the Red Line, was some five hundred yards further forward. The infantry resumed the attack at 6.45 am, following on behind the rolling barrage, which progressed in a series of jumps (75 yards initially, then 100 yards) providing a curtain of protective steel. This phase of the operation was more costly than the first, with the defending machine gunners and snipers putting up a fierce and determined defence. Despite this, and the temporary checks that were caused to parts of the advance, the objective was gained within the time limit allowed.

The problems for the Brigade came with the failure of 4th Division on the left. Much reduced in manpower, the two forward companies holding the Final Objective only had 110 men. They had made contact with the battalion on the right, but not with the Patricias on the left. It was not until almost midnight that a continuous line was formed, and

136

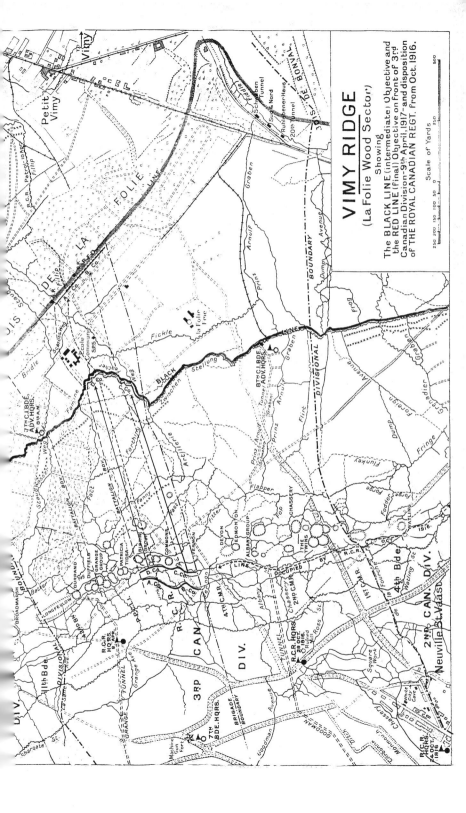

# VIMY RIDGE
## (La Folie Wood Sector)
### Showing

The BLACK LINE (Intermediate) Objective and the RED LINE (Final) Objective on Front of 3rd Canadian Division 9th April, 1917, and disposition of THE ROYAL CANADIAN REGT. from Oct. 1916.

Scale of Yards

250 200 150 100 50 0    250    500

this required the considerable reinforcement of about seventy men from the 58th Battalion. The coming of night had spared the RCR from machine gun and sniper fire from Hill 145 which was to remain uncaptured until the next day.

## PRINCESS PATRICIA'S CANADIAN LIGHT INFANTRY

See Map
page 152

Immediately to the RCR's left was the PPCLI whose 250 yard front included the Duffield, Grange and Patricia-Tidsa group of craters, the part of the front which includes the preserved outpost systems. For some reason part of the Patricia-Tidsa group is marked Montreal; perhaps one of the craters was so named but on the trench map Montreal is well to the north, part of the Momber Group.

The first objective was the Famine trench system from the point where the Battalion met with the RCR to a major trench junction some three hundred yards to the north. This junction included two of the main German communication trenches from Petit Vimy to the north of the ridge - Beggar Trench went across Hill 145 and *Staubwasser Weg* connected up with Broadmarsh Crater. The capture of the position to the left by the neighbouring 4th Division, and most especially of Hill 145, was essential if 7 Brigade was to retain its objectives lower down the slope. This threat was to cause the PPCLI its greatest difficulties in

**Spoils of war: German prisoners being escorted to the waiting cages.**

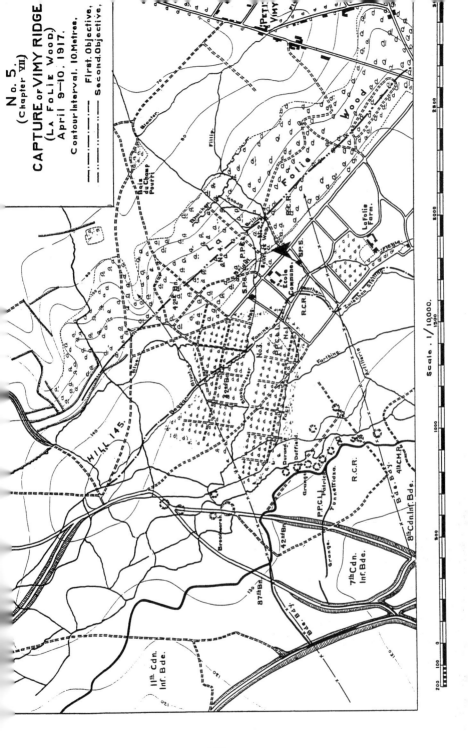

No. 5.
(Chapter VII)
CAPTURE of VIMY RIDGE
(LA FOLIE WOOD).
April 9-10, 1917.
Contour Interval. 10. Metres.

———————— First. Objective.
— · — · — Second. Objective.

Scale . 1/10,000.

139

A preserved German mortar position at the Canadian Memorial Park in the 1930s. Much of the 'hardware' was removed during the Second World War.

its assault on Vimy Ridge.

The initial attack was straight forward as the trench mortars had 'blown the garrisons and every shred of barbed wire sky high'. The crater line passed, the German front and support lines fell easily, the Bavarian defenders too befuddled by the bombardment to be able to resist. The first objective was reached and the assault made on the final objective on time. Orders made it clear that the most important task on completion of the attack was to consolidate the position along Bridle Trench and establish a Strong Point (No 6) on the *Staubwasser Weg*. The line of the 3rd Division by the end of the day would be on the eastern edge of the 130 metre plateau, looking down the steep slope towards Vimy and the green countryside beyond.

As the PPCLI progressed into La Folie Wood German opposition became stronger, Britt Trench proving a tough nut to crack. This trench was the link between the PPCLI and the RCR, and for a while both battalions' flanks were in the air. Eventually the trench was stormed after bombing the dug-outs and shooting point blank. Eighteen prisoners were taken, including four officers. The PPCLI had achieved their aim - and the Regimental historian comments on how this had been done.

It is a paradox, disconcerting to the historian, that complete success makes less history (in the case of small units at least) than

# BOIS EN HACHE—THE PIMPLE—HILL 145.

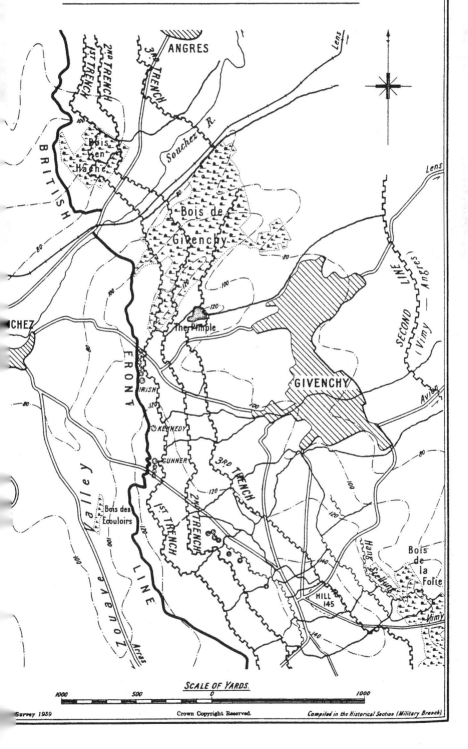

ANGRES

Bois en Hache

BRITISH

Souchez R.

Bois de Givenchy

The Pimple

SECOND LINE (Vimy — Angres)

GIVENCHY

IRISH

KENNEDY

GUNNER

Bois des Couloirs

FRONT LINE

Zouave Valley

3RD TRENCH

2ND TRENCH

1ST TRENCH

Hang Stellung

Bois de la Folie

HILL 145

Vimy

SCALE OF YARDS.

1000     500     0     1000

does failure or partial achievement. For the Patricias the great hour of the Vimy Ridge battle was the first, when they captured the whole of the two objectives allotted to them with less than fifty casualties. The very completeness with which a complicated chain of orders was carried out made it superfluous to set down the specific details of accomplishment. But it would be far from the truth to say that the storming of La Folie Wood was a walk over. It required not only the finest training and a scrupulous obedience to orders, but perfect leadership. Without good physique and the steadiest bearing no troops could have kept exact pace with the barrage in the 'hummocky waste' of craters and broken wire, as they went forward jumping from shell hole to shell hole under hot rifle and machine gun fire. It was an action to justify a commanding officer in the choice of his juniors for the leaders were bound to fall. ...The whole business of organizing the intermediate objective was at one time in the hands of one sergeant, while another took charge of the consolidation of SP 6.'

The hours after the attack were taking their toll in casualties, with snipers from Hill 145 causing severe difficulty. The failure of the 4th Division attack meant that the 42nd Battalion, on the Patricias left, had to refuse its flank and dig a trench from the jumping off point to the new front line. This meant that the Patricias had to extend their line to the left to take over much of the burden from the 42nd who had in turn to guard an unanticipated extra 1200 yards of front. As the day progressed German air superiority became a problem as it was able to direct artillery fire on to the new line. Casualties mounted and the artillery became so devastating that SP No 6, completed at the cost of considerable toil and sweat, was flattened and had to be abandoned. The Battalion suffered 160 casualties in the twenty four hours between 10.30 am April 9th to 10.30 am April 10th - over three times its losses in the initial assault. German attacks were threatened from the north and the east as April 9th progressed. Troops were seen massing on Hill 145 at 3.30 pm and officers were noticed around 4 pm on horseback riding behind Bracken trench organizing an attack. The pressure was relieved by the capture of Hill 145 during the afternoon of April 10th and by the evening of April 11th the Patricias were on their way to the rear and their billets at Villers au Bois.

## THE 46th (SOUTH SASKATCHEWAN) BATTALION CEF

This battalion was in 10 Brigade and in reserve for the the 4th Division attack on Hill 145 on April 9th. Only a week or so before the

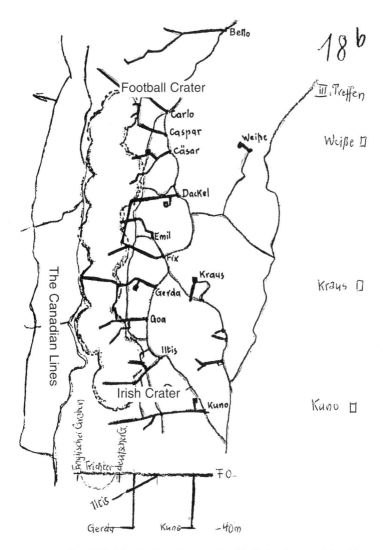

German shafts on The Pimple (Five Crossroads) with the heads named. See Map on Page 53.

attack this brigade had been given the additional task of capturing the Pimple, which was originally to have taken place twenty four hours after the southern part of the operation against Vimy Ridge had been completed.

Hill 145 was the dominant point on Vimy Ridge giving clear views over the British lines to the west along the Souchez Valley and Zouave Valley to the south west, as well as to the reserve positions beyond. In allied hands it would offer tremendous views over the Plain of Douai and the rear German positions around Lens and Vimy Ridge itself would be under direct observation. It was a key feature. The German defences were strong not only in lines of trenches and the redoubt into which Hill 145 was turned but also with tunnels, which formed part of the mine workings, and deep dug-outs in the Hang Stellung on the eastern side of the ridge which provided cover for the garrison and the reserve companies. Preparations for the attack were largely undisturbed by the enemy. The reason for this seems to be that the Germans were planning a limited attack of their own to remove the Canadians from their positions at the northern end of Zouave Valley thereby giving them complete control of the valley and hindering any attempts to take the Ridge. The allies got their attack in first. 12 Brigade was to seize Hill 145 and 11 Brigade the ground to the left, extending its control to the edges of Givenchy. In the attack the left flank of 12 Brigade's attack broke down, and although the summit was taken, the 54th Battalion was forced to withdraw when it came under sustained flanking fire from its right. The situation was difficult, with only 102nd Battalion on its position, the south eastern slope of the hill. By evening the Germans had been removed from the summit, although the situation was still fraught with danger as the Germans were still holding the reserve position, the *Hang Stellung*. 12 Brigade suffered from two directions - from the right, because of the failure to take the summit, and the Pimple on the left where the Germans had a clear view of the Canadians once the smoke screen and snowstorm had cleared.

46th Battalion sent up two companies to assist by helping to clear the Germans from a number of craters on the north west side of Hill 145. However the situation remained unresolved because of the Germans hold to the right. The only solution was for 11 Brigade's job to be completed by the 44th and 50th Battalions of 10 Brigade, which relieved the exhausted men of 11 Brigade who had been attempting to capture and then cling on to their first objectives. On April 10th these two battalions took the Red Line objectives of the first day, so enabling 12 Brigade to complete its operations. 46th Battalion carried out its part of the operation by sending men to establish outposts in Basin and Cyanide trenches and to exploit them in line with the rest of the attack. Only a small proportion of the battalion was directly involved in this attack and it suffered relatively few casualties.

If the situation was now stable to the south of Hill 145, the Pimple still posed a threat to the success of the operation. Therefore, as planned, 10 Brigade launched its attack upon the Pimple on April 12th, the 46th Battalion being on the left flank. In preparation for the assault the artillery blasted reserve areas and communication trenches, and the Royal Engineers fired a number of canisters of gas by Lievens projectors into Givenchy, aiming to catch German soldiers sheltering in the cellars of buildings. At 5 am the attack was launched, and again the Canadians had the advantages of wind in their backs and driving snow blinding the enemy. The appalling weather also lulled the Germans into a false sense of security, confident that no-one would attempt an attack in such conditions. Only on the 46th front was there effective opposition in the early phase of the battle.

'We hadn't gone three or four steps when the little fellow who loaded the rifle grenades for me had his head blown off. I was looking right at him and all of a sudden his head just vanished. I had bits of his brain scattered all over my tunic.' (Sgt N McLeod)

The battalion faced greatest resistance as it went over the crest, but fortunately the snowstorm prevented them from being good targets. By 7 am the battalion had secured its flank and the Pimple was captured

**Time to rest after the battle.**

except for a small post on the Souchez-Givenchy road between the 44th and 73rd Battalions which pulled back in the course of the day. During the night 46th Battalion was left in charge of the hill and by the afternoon of the following day, the 13th, began to prod forward cautiously into Angres. Its attack on the Pimple cost the battalion 108 casualties, 26 fatal. Soon after the battle the battalion erected two crosses on the Pimple one with the names of those killed on April 9th and the other those killed on April 12th. These survived for some years, but there no longer remains any trace of them. The only remaining memorial to the fighting that took place on the Pimple is the concrete surrounds of the 44th (Manitoba) Battalion memorial. The cross and panel with the names was taken back to Winnipeg in 1926.

## 72nd BATTALION
## (SEAFORTH HIGHLANDERS OF CANADA) CEF

See Map
page 152
+ 157

The 72nd Battalion was in 12 Brigade, the 4th Division. On the evening of April 7th it moved into the shelter of Gobron Tunnel. As for others waiting in the subways, they were able to enjoy the benefit of hot soup and other refreshments before moving out to their assault positions. The 72nd was a severely depleted unit, having an attacking strength of only 400, just over half what other battalions were generally able to make available. Its job was to act as the left flank of the whole attack onto the final objective.

The move into the jumping off trenches was delayed until 5 am; the assault was preceded by the firing of two mines under the German lines to the right of their front. The German barrage came down heavily, particularly over the left of the battalion front, in the vicinity of Montreal Crater, whilst heavy machine gun fire poured across from the Pimple. A difficulty shared by many of the battalions was the problem of keeping direction over the shell and crater scarred terrain. Heavy fighting took place in the triangle formed by Clutch and Cluck trenches. Whilst this was being attacked frontally a group of three men, Lt D Vicars and two soldiers worked their way around to the right flank of Clutch Trench.

'Armed chiefly with bombs which they manipulated with unerring efficiency, the three proceeded to take, unaided, about 400 yards of the strongly held German support line. Slipping from traverse to traverse along the trench, the dauntless trio advanced, clearing or partially clearing each bay by throwing bombs into it before entering and finishing the job with revolver and cold steel. Time after time Boches braver and more cunning than the rest attempted to waylay them by lying in wait in the

146

doorways of their dug-outs, only to be met by a courage more deadly than their own. Pushing the now thoroughly demoralised Boches before them, the three continued their advance [*northwards*] until practically the whole trench on the Battalion front was cleared. Aided by the arrival of the frontal attacking troops they drove the completely routed Bavarians to their destruction in the heavy 'standing barrage', which was protecting the left flank of the attack.'

Eventually the battalion achieved its objectives, but only 62 of its men who went over the top on April 9th were not casualties. During the night fresh troops were brought up from Gobrun Tunnel, whilst reconnaissance showed that the Germans were installed in Claude trench two hundred yards or so to the east. Once the Pimple had been captured and the bloody irritant of its snipers and machine guns removed, the battalion proceeded with its advance, removing the defenders from Claude Trench and pressing on to Givenchy. Later on the morning of April 13th the CO and the Brigade commander (Brig Gen JH MacBrien) found themselves right out in front of their own men to the north east of the village. Seeing a large body of Germans who seemed to be dithering as to what to do, they opened fire with their revolvers and saw them off. Advancing Canadians, some five hundred yards away, did not recognize the pair and opened fire, wounding the Brigadier in the arm.

The German Army had been thoroughly defeated, not least because its local commander had misread the situation. General von Falkenhausen had imagined that the attack on Vimy Ridge would produce a Somme type battle, a long drawn out campaign of attrition based on the original German defences. He used his reserve divisions not to counter attack but as a source of manpower to hold the line. The decision was fatal to the German chances of holding the Ridge and they would never possess it again in the war.

General Horne, First Army commander, summarised the reasons for the success of the Canadian Corps succinctly.

'The Vimy Ridge has been considered as a position of very great strength; the Germans have considered it to be impregnable. To have carried this position with so little loss testifies to the soundness of plan, thoroughness of preparation, dash and determination in execution, and devotion to duty on the part of all concerned.'

Vimy Ridge had greater implications than just a military victory, spectacular though it was. For the first time the Canadian divisions had gone into action side by side - in effect as a national army. The victory

147

made Canadians far more conscious of their own identity and place in the world. Byng had followed a policy of replacing British officers in senior and staff appointments with Canadians and on June 9th 1917 he handed over command of the Corps to the highly successful Canadian, General Currie. It was not to be the end of Byng's connection with Canada, for he became Governor General from 1921 - 1926.

The Canadian Corps remained amongst the best of the shock troops the British forces could put in the field, with perhaps its finest hour coming in the series of battles in 1918 marking the defeat of Germany. But it is Vimy Ridge that has lingered in Canadian national consciousness.

**Left: General Byng.**

**Below: Canadian Brigade Headquarters after the battle**

# Bibliography

*Official History France and Belgium 1917* Vol 1. Compiled by Capt C Falls.

*The Canadian Expeditionary Force 1914 - 1919.* Col GWL Nicholson. Ottowa 1962.

*Byng of Vimy.* J Williams. Leo Cooper 1983.

*The Journal of Private Fraser 1914 - 1918.* ed RH Roy. Sono Nis Press 1985.

*Gunner Ferrguson's Diary.* ed PG Rogers. Lancelot Press 1985.

*Gallant Canadians - The story of the Tenth Canadian Infantry Battalion 1914 - 1919.* DG Dancocks. Penguin Books Canada Ltd. 1990.

*History of the 16th Battalion (Canadian Scottish) CEF 1914 - 1919.* HM Urquhart. MacMillan (Canada) Ltd. 1932.

*The 13th Battalion Royal Highlanders of Canada 1914 -1919.* RC Featherstonhaugh. By the Regiment.

*1925 From the Rideau to the Rhine and Back - 6th Field Company and Battalion in the Great War.* K Weatherbe. Hunter-Rose Co. 1928.

*Royal Canadian Regiment 1883 - 1933.* RC Featherstonhaugh. By the Regt. 1936.

*Princess Patricia's Canadian Light Infantry 1914 - 1919.* Vol 1. R Hodder-Williams. Hodder and Stoughton. 1923.

*The Suicide Battalion.* JL McWilliams and RJ Steel. Vanwell Publishing Ltd. 1990.

*History of the 72nd Canadian Infantry Battalion Seaforth Highlanders of Canada.* B McEvoy and Capt AH Finlay. Cowan & Brookhouse 1920.

# TOUR OF THE AREA

**I would most strongly recommend that the reader purchases the IGN 2406 Est ARRAS before commencing this part of the tour - it will make life so much easier, not least in transposing the trench map extracts onto a modern Ordnance Survey type equivalent.**

It is possible to have a very lengthy walk around the whole area but this would probably come to twenty five miles or so - good luck to the energetic! As for all battlefield tours the ideal is a coach that can drop off people at Point A and collect from Point B. The same can of course be achieved by the use of two cars. It is probably the most comfortable way of carrying out an effective tour of a battlefield area, because in the end nothing can compare with walking the ground which, after all, is how the soldiers had to do it at the time.

For the purposes of this guide I have come up with seven different tours that take into account accessibility and the division of the ground caused by the autoroute and other man-made obstacles rather than the logic of the battles and engagements as they unfurled.

1. **The Pimple or Five Crossroads (German)**
2. **Zouave Valley**
3. **The Canadian Memorial Park**
4. **La Folie Farm and La Justice**
5. **Lichfield**
6. **Neuville St Vaast Southern sector**
7. **La Targette**

VIMY

SOUCHEZ

CIVENCHY
EN-GOHELLE

NEUVILLE
ST-VAAST

Broadmarsh
Crater

S B Clough

0   500   1000
M

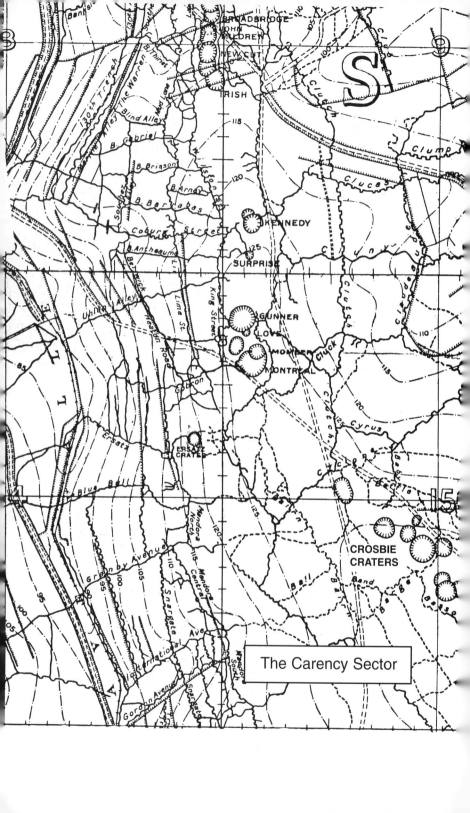

The Carency Sector

# 1. The Pimple or Five Crossroads (German)

Access is **via Souchez**, following the signposts to **Givenchy-en-Gohelle Canadian Cemetery**. Immediately after the motorway bridge **turn left** and follow the road until it is blocked. From here walk across the field to the concrete remains of the 44th Battalion CEF Memorial. Good views may be had from this area of Givenchy to the east, Souchez and the Lorette Spur to the west and along Zouave Valley to the south. Accounts of what happened on this part of the ridge will be found in Chapters 1,2,3 and 8.

The craters in this area have, for the most part, been filled in. At the time of the Canadian Corps attacks staff officers

The remnants of the 44th Bn Memorial

went down to the old Somme Battlefield to examine the heavily cratered (and shelled) ground there and compared conditions with those on the ridge. The craters on the Somme were categorised according to the type of crater and the sort of obstacle that it created. Thus categories included the Fricourt Group, the Carnoy Group, Lochnagar Crater and Y Sap Crater. They also looked at the Somme craters to see what sort of possibilities they might offer for the concealing and moving of men. This was a vital process as the whole of the Ridge was lined with craters. Comments on the craters and their comparison with those on the Somme are taken from the Canadian Corps Scheme of Operations (hereinafter called the scheme of operations or the scheme).

Irish to Football Craters were said to,

'resemble the La Boisselle Group blown at about the same depth, forming a crater group averaging 30 feet in depth by 90 feet across, with a number of causeways between craters. It should be quite possible to cross this group with about 7 parties of 6 to 8 men each. Each party should be able to negotiate the sides of a crater, taking advantage of any existing causeways.'

The La Boisselle Group (better known as the Glory Hole) is still in existence and may be seen on the western edge of that village.

About 200 yards due south of the Memorial was Kennedy Crater,

153

which stood on its own and was 'possibly better avoided'. For the attack on April 9th it was intended to fire a mine to the rear of the crater to remove the German defenders who might not have been destroyed by the barrage. 150 to 200 yards south of Kennedy was the Gunner to Montreal Craters, which group included Love and Momber. At the moment, for some reason, Montreal is marked as over by the preserved trench area. It was here. The Corps Scheme commented,

'Montreal Crater resembles Y Sap Crater [*until the early 1970s this could be seen on the north side of the Albert - Bapaume road near the La Boisselle Communal Cemetery*] and is smaller than Lochnagar Crater. Both Y Sap (59 feet deep by 200 feet across) and Lochnagar (55 feet by 280 feet across) can be crossed but only by small parties slowly. Probably 2 or 3 parties of 6 to 8 men each could get through this group'.

**Returning to the car**, drive to Givenchy-en-Gohelle Cemetery and park. The road has now been brought alongside the cemetery - hitherto there was a walk of over 100 yards from a road that has now gone.

Montreal Crater was about 120 yards north west of the cemetery. Follow the muddy track alongside the cemetery eastwards. Behind the barbed wire and in the wooded area the battlefield has been left largely untouched, and it is quite possible that the Crosbie Group of Craters has survived. These are some 250 yards away from the cemetery and about fifty yards into the wood, stretching off in a line in a south easterly direction.

**Remnants of a trench, possibly Uhlan Alley.**

Return to your car and **drive back towards Souchez**; about three hundred yards after the motorway underpass look on your left hand side at the ground dropping away. A very clear zig-zag trench line may be seen. This is possibly the remnants of Uhlan Alley, a communication trench. Some yards further on, just before a slight kink in the road to the left, was the entrance to Coburg Subway, which ran from here in an east north easterly direction for 445 yards towards (but well short of) Kennedy Crater.

154

Zouave Valley from the west looking across the new motorway which slices its way along the west side of Vimy Ridge.

Proceed into the eastern outskirts of Souchez and take the left turning marked with a CWGC sign to **Zouave Valley Cemetery**.

## 2.  Zouave Valley

There are frequent references to Zouave Valley throughout the book but Chapters 2, 3 and 4 are particularly important, as well as the latter part of Chapter 1.  Drive towards Zouave Valley Cemetery; after about 800 yards, just before a right kink in the road look east.  Just short of the motorway was the entrance to the Gobron Subway. Rather closer from this position, about 200 yards away to the south east was the entrance to the Blue Bull Subway which ran between Ersatz and Blue Bull trenches. Continue towards the cemetery - about 50 - 100 yards short of it, by the roadside, was the entrance to Vincent Subway, with Vincent Street itself running off east from the cemetery.

We are now just to the rear of where some of the heaviest fighting took place during the German attack of May 21st 1916. Take the metalled **road to the right** which leads to the *Chemin des Pylones* (or

Looking down the valley towards Souchez from Zouave Valley Cemetery.

The Chemin des Pylones at the Souchez end.

the Music Hall Line). **Turn right** and drive along for a few yards. There are good views of the cemetery and the *Talus des Zouaves* to the left, although the views to the ridge itself are obstructed by the motorway. Proceed along this road so far as you might wish - it was the French line for some time in 1915, and it was the British emergency line in due course.

A careful examination of the sketch map accompanying the Brigade Major's Diary is recommended whilst here to locate all the various dumps and HQs that he has marked. Wherever convenient turn around and **return to the cemetery** and take the track alongside the embankment; I have found this passable with care in a car in January. Should you not wish to risk this, return to Souchez and pick the track

Coming from Neuville St Vaast the road branches: to the left is Chemin des Pylones, to the right towards Zouve Valley Cemetery and the Talus des Zouaves.

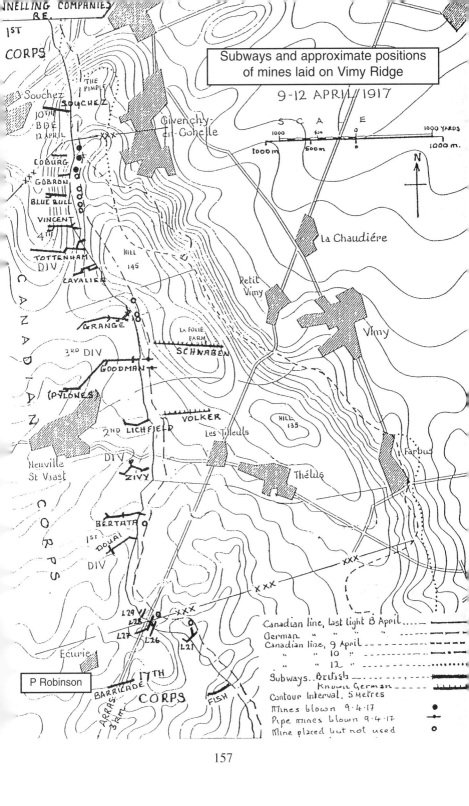

Subways and approximate positions
of mines laid on Vimy Ridge

9-12 APRIL 1917

SCALE

P Robinson

157

up from the Neuville St Vaast end. Coming from the cemetery proceed for about a kilometre (the surface improves dramatically after a few hundred yards). 300 yards or so before the road turn sharply to the left by the side of the road (or possibly buried by the motorway) is the entrance of Grange Subway.

Continuing **towards Neuville** either take the metalled road into the town and come back out onto the Chemin des Pylones or follow the track which I have found quite passable which brings the tourer out at a forked junction, the right being the Chemin des Pylones, the left running in to Neuville. At the fork look due west about a hundred yards into the field - this is the site of the entrance for Goodman Subway, the longest of the thirteen subways. It emerged 1883 yards later near Chassery Crater which is in the woodland to the east as the motorway is crossed on the Givenchy Road. Goodman Subway was connected with Pylones Subway which had been dug to protect men coming from the west who were otherwise exposed as they went over the rise in the ground. Proceed into Neuville St Vaast and take the road to the Vimy memorial and Givenchy.

## 3. The Canadian Memorial Park

For this section of the tour Chapters 2 and 3 are relevant and of particular interest are Chapters 4, 5, 7 and part of 8.

Shortly after crossing the motorway take a sharp **backward turn to the left**. Before progressing too far down this road be warned that it can

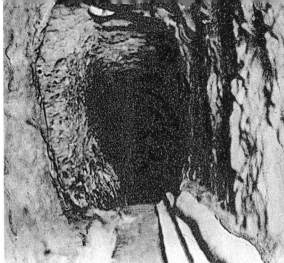

**Left: Tunnel entrance. Right: Part of Grange Tunnel in the early post-war days.**

See Map page 152 + 179

be very difficult to find a place to turn around, especially in muddy conditions or if the fields are planted. It might be wiser to spend an hour or so walking this part of the route. This little road runs along the eastern side of the motorway and it is possible to have excellent views across much of the fighting described in most of the chapters in the book. After about 300 yards running alongside the autoroute the road crosses Lassalle Avenue. Snargate Street ran parallel in the fields to the right. Other famous trenches are passed - Cavalier, Central, and Tottenham. The track deteriorates and makes its way into the German lines of April 1917, but the continuations of Vincent Street and Gordon and International Avenues are passed. It was here, to the north west of Canadian Cemetery No.2 that so much of the heavy fighting of May 21st 1916 took place.

**Return to the main road** and turn into the car park for the tunnel and preserved trenches.

There was originally no intention of opening up a tunnel and deliberately preserving some of the trenches when the project to build the Vimy Memorial began in 1926. However, the Canadian Engineers delegated to work on the task spent part of their spare time wandering around the battlefield, and the entrance to the Grange tunnel was found covered over by brush. It was explored and found to be in good condition and the decision was made that a section of the outpost lines of both sides and a section of subway would be open to the public as a part of the Memorial complex.

Thousands of people now come and visit the Memorial, a stop made

159

British sentry positions

Hartkopf Crater blown on the 26th July, 1916, with 11,000 pounds of explosives producing a crater forty yards across and twenty yards deep. Photo top was taken the next day and shows white walls caused by the chalk. View taken from the German to the British crater sentry. This is a British steel cover with a loophole between sandbags. The photo below is taken from the same position some three weeks later - notice the significant colour change in the surface of the crater and the British position. This crater is about 150 yards north of Broadmarsh, to the right of the Vimy Memorial road. See Map page 118.

British sentry positions

easy even for the casual visitor because of the close proximity of the
main autoroute to Paris. The best time to come is earlyish in the
morning, before the hordes descend which they do from about 11 am
onwards, certainly in the summer months. The preserved trenches do
look artificial, but they were recreated by veterans of the war who used
the original trench line and sandbags filled with concrete. The
indentations of the sandbag can be seen quite clearly on the concrete

The Grange Subway, top and left in the post-war years and below, in a rather safer condition, recently.

A German sapper on the lip of Noyon Crater, early 1917

See Map page 118

163

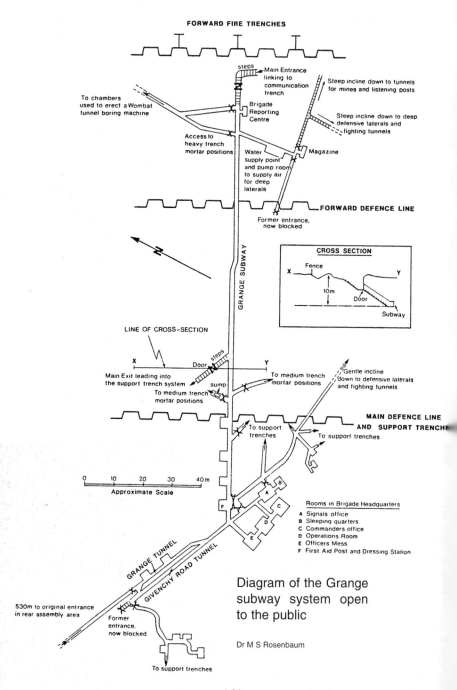

**FORWARD FIRE TRENCHES**

steps — Main Entrance linking to communication trench

Steep incline down to tunnels for mines and listening posts

To chambers used to erect a Wombat tunnel boring machine

Brigade Reporting Centre

Steep incline down to deep defensive laterals and fighting tunnels

Access to heavy trench mortar positions

Water supply point and pump room to supply air for deep laterals

Magazine

**FORWARD DEFENCE LINE**

Former entrance, now blocked

GRANGE SUBWAY

LINE OF CROSS-SECTION

### CROSS SECTION

X — Fence

10m — Door

Y

Subway

X — Door — steps — Y

Main Exit leading into the support trench system

sump

To medium trench mortar positions

To medium trench mortar positions

Gentle incline down to defensive laterals and fighting tunnels

**MAIN DEFENCE LINE AND SUPPORT TRENCH**

To support trenches

To support trenches

0  10  20  30  40m
**Approximate Scale**

A

B

C

F

D

E

**Rooms in Brigade Headquarters**
A Signals office
B Sleeping quarters
C Commanders office
D Operations Room
E Officers Mess
F First Aid Post and Dressing Station

GRANGE TUNNEL

GIVENCHY ROAD TUNNEL

530m to original entrance in rear assembly area

Former entrance, now blocked

To support trenches

## Diagram of the Grange subway system open to the public

Dr M S Rosenbaum

blocks that have remained. What is perhaps unfortunate is that the trenches are not usual for other parts of the Western Front, for what has been preserved is the outpost line of both sides. These positions were lightly held, on the lips of craters and were designed to act as watchposts against enemy attacks or raids. They differ, therefore, from usual front line positions in the number of saps that they have, for example and other aspects of trench construction are inevitably different. The main British/Canadian position here was a couple of hundred yards to the rear, by the exit of the public part of the Grange Subway. The German line opposite served a similar purpose, and likewise its main position was some distance further back.

The craters give a graphic idea of how battered the ground of Vimy Ridge had become by April 9th 1917. To the south (to the British right) the craters are somewhat misleadingly labelled. I would conjecture that Winnipeg should be labelled Patricia Crater, and that to the right is certainly Tidsa. Further off and not far into the woods (but fenced off) are the Birkin Group and Commons Craters about which the scheme of operations comments,

> 'are smaller than even the Fricourt Group [the craters known as the Triple Tambour, still extant above Fricourt] and form no serious obstacle to advance over.'

In front of the preserved trenches are the Grange and Duffield (not Du Field as indicated by the Notice Board) Groups of Craters. These look quite impressive but the authors of the scheme of operations were quite dismissive about them, saying that they resembled,

> 'the La Boisselle Group and could be crossed by 8 parties of

Part of the Tidsa Group of craters as they appear today.

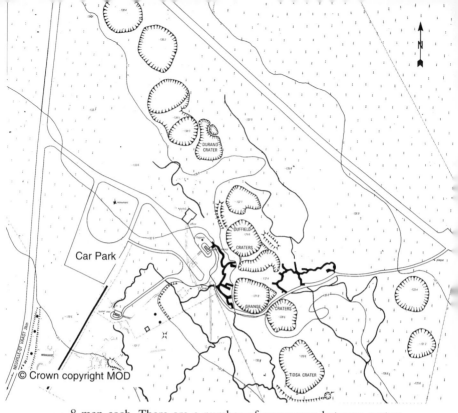

© Crown copyright MOD

8 men each. There are a number of causeways between craters and the craters themselves are nowhere insurmountable.'

To the north is Durand Crater (behind the Reception Building) which the staff had considered blowing on April 9th but which in the end they decided not to do. The scheme commented that it resembled,

'the Fricourt Craters and like them has a large amount of clay. Is possible to cross, but bottom would be very wet in wet weather and should be skirted.'

Beyond Durand is a line of craters known as Longfellow. The Germans had become increasingly concerned about the very obvious works being done by tunnellers on the Ridge and it was evident that they returned some of their own tunnellers to the ridge, especially from this point northwards, to engage in defensive mining operations. Lt Col GE Williams RE, Inspector of Mines in the First Army submitted a report shortly after the April 9th attack on Mining Operations on the Arras front and his text explains the circumstances surrounding operations between Durand and Broadmarsh Craters. Durand is marked on the large scale map; Broadmarsh is the large crater just north of the fork in the Givenchy road.

'Throughout the preparatory stage the enemy had shown

166

intermittent activity in the Grange-Durand cratered area. He had blown two or three times, though without doing us any serious damage, and was working at several places on this front till the last. A few days before April 9th he blew a group of 9 mines, the craters of which were continuous and closed the gap between Durand and Broadmarsh Craters, except for a width of 100 yards. This combined crater was named Longfellow. It was thereupon decided to abandon the defilading mine [*ie a mine that would secure the attack from the enfilading fire from the German positions on Broadmarsh*] on the grounds that its crater would completely close the gap through which the assaulting infantry must pass to their objective. The position of Broadmarsh Crater is very commanding, and situated as it is at the commencement of a re-entrant in the enemy lines, it completely enfiladed our position behind the main group of craters to the south. It is a question whether the abandonment of this mine was wise, for our troops suffered heavily in traversing the gap. An inspection of Broadmarsh Crater has shown that the enemy dug-outs at the bottom were practically untouched by the bombardment. There is every reason to believe that the enemy machine gunners accommodated in them were ready on the lip when the assault came over.'

Whilst here at Broadmarsh it would be as well to re-read the accounts of Jones VC and the part played in the area by Major Johnston in Chapters 5 and 4 respectively. A couple of the craters north of Broadmarsh were fired defensively in the spring of 1917. Whilst here it

would be as well to walk down to the two cemeteries signposted to the left, though it is possible to park a car next to them when the road has not been chained off.

**Return to the Reception Building**. On first arriving you should check here the times and availability of places for a visit to the Tunnel. The guide book is sufficient for an explanation of the tunnel system, so it does not matter if you end up going on a French tour. Try and book yourself a place so that you can use any time waiting visiting other points of interest in this part of the Memorial Park. The visits are every half hour and last about thirty to forty minutes. It can be quite chilly underground, especially noticeable on a hot summer's day, and in wet weather there is a tendency for it to 'rain' through the roof, so dress accordingly. The subway is open to visitors, conditions underground allowing, from mid April to mid November and the tour is free.

The subway was constructed between November 1916 and March 1917. Although at the end of the day all the subways were used for the same purposes - the safeguarding and passage of men, the provision of Dressing Stations, routes for signals wire and water pipes and water storage - they were originally envisaged to have varying uses. One division aimed to use them entirely for signallers, signals and signals equipment. Another was to use them for the storage of men and ammunition and for the housing of brigade and battalion staffs; or for communications to trench mortar emplacements, storage of ammunition and accommodation of the crews. The present day system has been improved by reinforcing the supports and making the passageways rather higher and wider, as well as increasing the power of the lighting considerably.

When the subways were built they were additions to pre-existing systems, such as fighting trenches, trench mortar emplacements and defensive listening posts. The subways were also interconnected by deep tunnels known as laterals. These were primarily designed to provide an equivalent of the front line underground, and to prevent German mining activities under the British lines. They were also used for ventilation and access. Some of the subways were driven forward at the last moment so that troops could emerge directly into No Man's Land. They all had a number of entrances/exits in case any of these should be shelled and destroyed.

On completing this tour **return to the car** and head north towards the memorial and:

## 4. La Folie Farm and La Justice

**Turn right** after a few yards at the road junction and proceed for about a mile. Tucked away on the left hand side of the road there is a gate through the wiring around the forest with a notice above, 3rd Division Memorial. 300 yards further on, as the road turns sharply left, there is a track coming from the right. It is usually practicable to park the car here. **Return to the gate** and walk along the path, **bearing right** after a hundred yards or so, The Divisional Memorial, in the shape of a cross, is in a small clearing surrounded by the forest. This is the site of La Folie Farm. The ground round about shows the ravages of war with shell holes in abundance and trenches crisscrossing the wood.

It is possible to visit the memorial via the walk through the forest near the car park at la Justice.

**Return to your car.** The track leads eventually to Neuville St Vaast (this was part of the old road from Neuville to Petit Vimy) and to the area covered by Tour 5. The track is impassable at one or two points to anything but a four wheel drive vehicle. Proceed along the road as before and where the **road bends sharply to the right go straight on.** This road is metalled but badly pot-holed. It will bring you out after a short time to a large car parking area which is marked la Justice on the IGN map. The ground all about here shows definite signs of the ferocity of the struggle that took place almost eighty years ago.

**Proceed by foot into the Vimy Fores**t. Various trails off the main route will take you alongside shell holes and trenches (but the authorities are very keen that you stick to the trails and do not wander off). Along here was the Ecole Commune, about two thirds of the way down where the track turns slightly to the right. Soon after the pathway comes out to the south of the Vimy Memorial. Another trail (to the left) will take you to the 3rd Division memorial. The maps provided with the sections on the PPCLI and the RCR in Chapter 8 should enable the visitor to follow some of the action. On returning to the car park **follow a north easterly track** down the ridge towards Petit Vimy. When it emerges from the forest, about fifty yards or so in the field in front of you, is the Petit Vimy Cemetery, well worth a stop. The views across the plain of Douai are considerable.

Return to your car and to the main road, heading south east to the Lens - Arras road.

## 5. Lichfield

At the **junction turn right** and very soon Thelus Military Cemetery will be visible standing isolated in the open fields on your right. There is no obvious place to park your car, just draw off onto the verge which I have found to be quite sound even in wet weather. The path to the cemetery follows close to the line of *Grenadier Graben* and the cemetery itself was constructed in or close to Fry Trench, about 100 yards east of the main *Zwischen Stellung*. Proceed into Thelus (or Les Tilleuls as this western part was known in the war) and stop just before the traffic lights - it should be possible to mount the pavement. On the

170

opposite side of the road is the Canadian Corps Artillery Memorial which was dedicated in the presence of General Byng on April 9th 1918, this date according to a leading authority, the late Rose Coombs MBE. However, Canon Scott in his book *The Great War As I Saw It* reports the event differently.

'On February 19th, I held the dedication service at the unveiling of the artillery monument at Les Tilleuls. Owing to its exposed position no concourse of men was allowed, but there was a large gathering of the staff, including the Army Commander, and of course a number of officers from the artillery. The lines of the monument are very severe. A plain white cross surmounts a large mass of solid masonry on which is the tablet, which General Currie unveiled. It stands in a commanding position on Vimy Ridge, and can be seen for miles around. [*Alas, this is no longer true, and one has to look carefully to see it at all now!*] Many generations of Canadians in future ages will visit that lonely tribute to the heroism of those who, leaving home and loved ones, voluntarily came and laid down their lives in order that our country might be free.'

On the **right just before the traffic lights** there is a narrow road. It is possible to go along this to Lichfield Crater. If one wishes to be more orthodox, **turn right** at the traffic lights, **turn right** 150 yards after the Neuville St Vaast Communal Cemetery and come back over the motorway to the cemetery.

Assuming the first option has been taken, this is a road that existed during the war. Lichfield Crater was described as being useful for the attack on April 9th as: 'good to assemble men in; we have Sap into it'.

There is a some fairly firm grass on which to stop the car by the Crater Cemetery. About 100 yards to the right, and parallel with the road ran the German front line trench, Fringe. After the battle Lichfield subway was connected with the German Volker Tunnel about 200 yards to the south east. This ran from the road along which you have just driven into the *Zwischen Stellung*, not far from Thelus Military Cemetery. Proceeding, Watling Crater was to the left of the road just about where the wood commences on the right.

> *The scheme of operations commented that it was 'in the enemy front line. If blown trench is put across to it, it should help to form good communication'.*

**Litchfield Crater Cemetery from the air. The site of Watling Crater was in top left of the picture, in the trees to the left of the road.**

**Turn left over the motorway**. It is possible to stop the car just prior to this and walk up the track towards the site of La Folie Farm. Inside the northern part of the wood are the remnants of craters such as The Twins, Chassery and the Albany Group. In the field below is an isolated French tomb memorial. Once over the motorway bridge EITHER take a very **sharp turning to the left** or end this part of the tour in Neuville St Vaast by proceeding straight ahead. If taking the narrow turn, Lichfield Subway had its entrance in the fields about 200 yards SSW of the turning. Follow the track around and roughly midway between Lichfield and Zivy Cemeteries was Pulpit Crater described as 'a deep crater but not occupied by enemy on further side. Might be useful for assembling up to twenty men'. This road brings you out at:

## 6. Neuville St Vaast Southern Sector

For this section Chapters 1,6, 7 and 8 are most relevant.

**Turn left** and head for Zivy Crater Cemetery. This was described in the scheme as 'an isolated crater; would not form a serious obstacle'. Lt Col DE Macintyre knew the Crater from the war days and comments on it during the Vimy Pilgrimage which he helped to organise in 1936.

'I shall never forget the cemetery that was made in a large crater called the Zivy. It is just beside the road that connects Neuville St Vaast and Thelus. On Vimy Day it was a deep and slimy hole, half full of stinking water but today, thanks to the efforts of the CWGC, it has been transformed into a beautiful sunken garden....' [*The Vimy Pilgrimage, 1967*]

The farm track behind the crater cemetery runs along the old crater line for much of its course, running very close to the site of the Phillip Group ('old and shallow craters; no obstacle') and then moves just behind the old German front line and runs along it. A cemetery to the east is Nine Elms and beyond that near a new flyover is the Arras Road Cemetery. This road is not the easiest on which to turn around, and you might have to reverse the whole way. It does give a good idea of what the soldier was seeing from the German point of view.

**Return to the Neuville St Vaast road** and take the **next turning left**. This track has been transformed into a highway, though at the time of writing it is not clear what this is for other than it has something to do with the upgrading of the Arras - Lens road. At the moment this is the only means of access to Arras Road Cemetery.

Along this road were a series of Company HQs (see London Scottish map in Chapter 6). Where the road forks (the right hand goes to the Communal Cemetery) there was a mill on the left. About two hundred yards due east of this was the Vissec Group of craters.

At this point it is worth while to divert **down the right hand fork** and visit the communal cemetery where the Canadian Corps achievement is commemorated on the village war memorial. This cemetery was heavily fought over by the French in 1915. A memorial may be seen on a high point (indicated by a few trees) on the horizon to the SSW. Returning the way you came, note the embankments and the possibilities they provided for shelter and dug-outs.

Rejoining the road, **head south**. After about **500 yard**s the Claudot

Group of craters was on the left. Some 250 yards and at a similar distance **on the right** was the Bentata Redoubt and the entrance to Bentata Subway. 250 yards before a turning to the right was the Paris Redoubt (both sides of the road); on the left hand side of the road, fifty yards or so into the fields, was the exit for the Douai Subway. This much improved track continues up to the Arras - Lens road; unfortunately the improvement seems to have removed all the remaining craters on the west side of that road.

**Turn right** along what was known as St Aubin Ditch, along the Notre Dame valley. Just before this, on the left hand side about fifty yards into the field, was the Argyll Group of craters. This road had a communication trench, Vase Avenue running just south of it and beyond that a tramway. Just before it comes to a crossroads, Fort B used to be on the right hand side.

At the **crossroads turn right**; to the left the road goes to Ecurie and the track opposite comes out on the Arras - Bethune Road at a point called Ariane, which was used as an Aid Post, Dump and had another cavern to hold troops. Further down this road but now a huge roundabout, was another dump and Aid Post, at Madagascar.

Having turned right the road becomes sunken, and the area was known as the Elbe Shelters and battalion HQs were located there. Off to the right and left was Fork Redoubt whose name came from the split in the road. Here is the memorial to Augustin Leuregans. Over to the west may be seen the line of trees that surrounds the huge German cemetery at Maison Blanche. The left hand fork fades away after a

**Displays of uniforms and equipment at the military museum at la Targette.**

hundred yards or more, so take the right hand road and head towards Neuville St Vaast. After a hundred yards Claudot Communication Trench is crossed, and 500 yards before it meets the Thelus road it crosses Territorial Avenue followed at 100 yard or so intervals by , Mercier, Guillermot and Rietz Avenue.

At the Thelus **road junction turn left** for Neuville St Vaast and make for:

## 7. La Targette

At the large cross in la Targette (the two villages run into each other) which is at a road junction, take the **right hand fork**. At the main road cross over and visit the museum if you have not already done so. Proceed south towards Arras and take the next right. Visit the British and French cemeteries and possibly have a drink and a bite to eat in the cafe on the corner. If you have an hour to spare enter the huge Au Rietz cavern on the east side of the Arras road. The commentary from the proprietor is quite lengthy, but it is quite an extraordinary place, capable of holding over 1,000 troops, though more chambers are being discovered all the time. These caverns were used to provide stone for the building of Arras and the various fortifications that developed there over the centuries. Not only were foreign armies commonplace hereabouts, but the city itself was split into two factions from its earliest years. The great shaft which was used to lift the cut stone out of the quarries is an awesome sight in its own right.

**Proceed south a kilometr**e. On the left hand side is the vast German cemetery, Maison Blanche. There is no sign off the road, so be careful not to overshoot the entrance, which is at the northern edge (ie the La Targette end) of the cemetery. There are just under 45,000 buried in this graveyard, concentrated from all around the area, including a massive ossuary with over 8,000 in it. When I first visited this cemetery in 1968 when the crosses were wooden and there were twice as many of them (two names to a cross - now four names), they used to be stood in small flower beds. One of the four French gardeners at the time told me that there were sixty four kilometres of edging to be cut - more or less the

distance between Cambridge and north London.

On weekdays the comfortable and clean toilets of this cemetery are open.

This is the last place on the tour and no more suitable place could be found than here where lie the thousands of very professional German soldiers who had fought so tenaciously to hold their positions against the onslaught of the allies. It was their skill and determination that made the cost of pushing them back so expensive. The triumph of the British and Canadians, and the French before them was all the greater because they were such good soldiers.

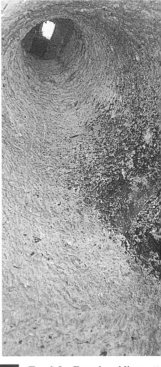

Top left: French soldiers in the village of La Targette early in the war.

Above: A 70 ft shaft used in the Middle Ages to remove quarried chalk.

Middle left: A cavern equipped for soldiers in the Labyrinth.

Left: Part of the underground caverns at Au Rietz today.

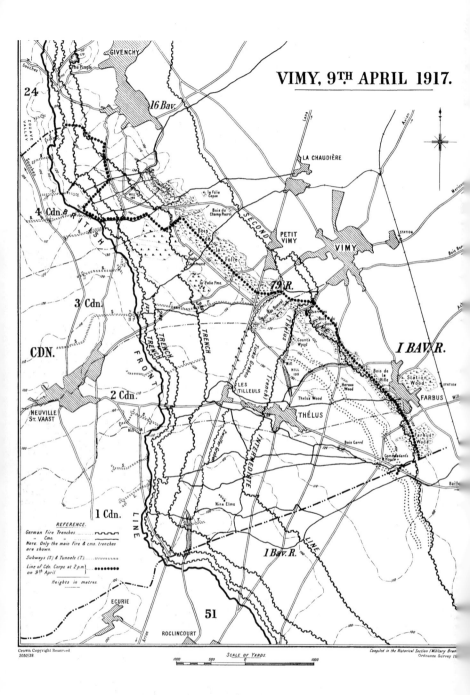

# VIMY, 9TH APRIL 1917.

REFERENCE.

German Fire Trenches ..........
  "          Cmn. ............
NOTE. Only the main Fire & cmn. trenches
are shown.

Subways (S.) & Tunnels (T.) ............

Line of Cdn. Corps at 2 p.m.
on 9th April ............

      Heights in metres.

SCALE OF YARDS

Compiled in the Historical Section (Military Bran...
Ordnance Survey 19...

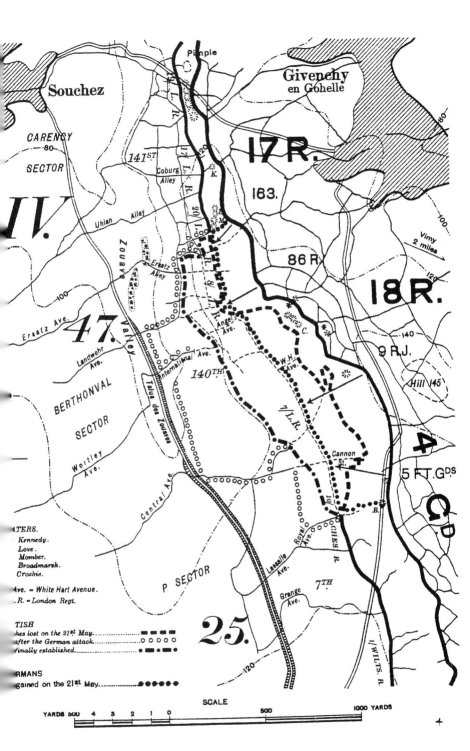

Souchez

Pimple

Givenchy
en Gohelle

CARENCY
SECTOR
80

141ST

Coburg
Alley

17 R.

163.

IV.

Uhlan Alley

Ersatz Ave.

47.

Zouave Valley

Ersatz Alley

K.

M.

86 R.

18 R.

9 R.J.

Vimy
2 miles

Angel Ave.

C.

Landwehr Ave.

International Ave.

140TH

W.H. Ave.

Hill 145

BERTHONVAL
SECTOR

Talus des Zouaves

7/L.R.

Wortley Ave.

Cannon St.

5 FT.G DS

Central Ave.

4
C D

ATERS.
Kennedy.
Love.
Momber.
Broadmarsh.
Crosbie.

Ave. = White Hart Avenue.
.R. = London Regt.

TISH
hes lost on the 21st May................
after the German attack............o o o o o
finally established..................●■·■·■·●

RMANS
gained on the 21st May...............●●●●●●

Royal Ave.

P SECTOR

Lasalle Ave.

Grange Ave.

7TH

1/WILTS. R.

25.

120

SCALE

YARDS 500   4   3   2   1   0          500          1000 YARDS

179

**Troops waiting to be bussed up to the line from Arras.**

## BEHIND THE LINE

This tour takes the visitor on a tour around some of the rear areas of the British army. The start point is the Maison Blanche German Cemetery.

**Proceed south** to the roundabout at the bottom of the Arras - Bethune road and take the first turning right. After a couple of kilometres take a **right turn** (D341) toward Maroeuil and Houdain.

See Map page 121

As the road climbs up, look left and right; tucked away in every fold of ground were batteries of artillery positioned for the bombardment on the ridge for April 9th. At the crossroads (left hand turn to Maroeuil) note the farm building on the right. This is the site of Brunehaut Farm. This road runs north eastwards to La Targette. It was one of the roads that suffered enormous strain in the days leading up to the April 9th attack; along one side there ran a tramway. This terminated at Birmingham Dump, near the entrance to Grange CT in Zouave Valley;

See Map page 65

another tramway, from Carency, terminated at Liverpool Dump.

At the *Cafe la Montagne* **turn right** along the D49 towards La Targette.

On the left hand side of the road was an RNAS (Royal Naval Air

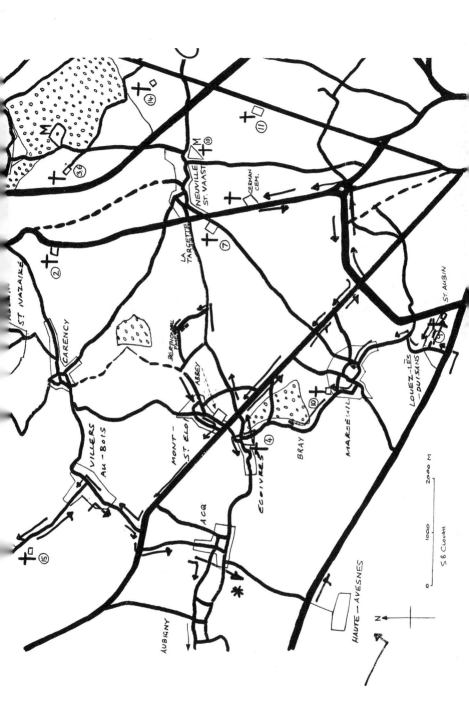

181

Top: Cafe la Montagne during 1915 with the twin towers of the ruined abbey in the background.
Bottom left: The Cafe today.
Bottom right: In front of the old airfield below the Abbey.

Service) airfield which stayed there for almost the whole of the war. It was tucked away under a couple of ridges safe from direct enemy observation, and the huge twin towers provided a clear reference point when it came to finding the airfield, no small consideration in the days before location beacons and radio communications. One of the commanding officers had the custom of flying between the towers of the ruined abbey on his return to the airfield - not quite as death defying a feat as it seems from a distance when one gets closer to the ruins, but dangerous nevertheless.

Take the **third turning on the left**, towards a farm building in some trees. This is Berthonval Farm, and a look at the artillery map for the attack on Vimy Ridge will show how the whole of this area was covered in guns. Byng had his forward Headquarters in the farm just before and during the battle. An account of life in the Farm during these days comments on how the noise of staff officers boots on bare

See Map page 121

Berthonval Farm, Byng's forward HQ during the battle for the Ridge in 1917.

floorboards rung out; one wonders how anyone heard anything with the incessant row that the guns must have made in the fortnight before April 9th. Note the large wood (straight ahead before you turn), Berthonval Wood, which was a forming up place for the French 77th Division for its attack on May 9th. It is possible to walk from the wood along paths to Zouave Valley. The wood itself still shows signs of having been knocked about. Just to the right of Berthonval Farm was where the Moroccan Division formed up and set off on their attack.

**Turn left** towards Mont St Eloi which was often used as a Brigade Headquarters. Stop by the ruined abbey. Its condition is variously blamed on the 16th century French Wars of Religion, the Franco-Spanish wars of the 17th century, the French Revolution or the Franco-Prussian War. The French Revolution seems to be the most likely. There is a viewing platform in the southern tower, but the entrance to

Looking at Mont St Eloi from the northwest. Off to the right of the picture is Ecoivres.

this seems to be permanently locked. Going forward from the tower there are good views over the valley which must have presented an extraordinary spectacle of activity and fire-power in the first days of April. Troops were strictly forbidden to loiter on this forward edge of Mont St Eloi.

On returning to the main road (D341) **turn right** and after a few kilometres **turn right again** (D58) to Villers au Bois. Towards the far end of the village **take the D65** which will have a CWGC sign to Villers Station cemetery, which is about two kilometres north west of the village. In the fields round about were billets for many of the troops who were out of the line. At the end of a line of trees, concealed in a wood, is the *Chateau de la Haie*, which was used by numerous divisions and higher formations as a Headquarters. Proceeding further along this road, the driver will come to Servins in the fields around which some of the battalions carried out their detailed rehearsals for the attack on April 9th. **Return to** Villers au Bois and the main road (D341) **turning right** and then **immediately left** for Acq. This was a typical quiet village (Private Fraser complained that there was nothing of interest in it), but it did house the Concert Party of various divisions, most notably the 51st (Highland) which was popular even with Private Fraser.

This part adds some distance, and the driver may wish to move straight to the part of the tour marked with an *.

Proceed from here **along the D49** to Aubigny via Frevin Capelle. Aubigny was the rail head for supplies coming in from the UK. It was also the home of the Crater Consolidation School and the Sniping School amongst various other specialist training centres set up by the

**Frequently used as a divisional headquarters, the stately chateau at Hermaville.**

various Corps and Army commands behind the lines. It was also the base for a Casualty Clearing Station.

From Aubigny head south on the D74 to Hermaville. Behind the church in that village is a magnificent chateau, used by various divisions as an Headquarters, amongst them the 60th. A tremendous amount of hot air has been expended on the subject of staff officers resting secure in their chateau whilst Tommy Atkins shivered and suffered deprivation in the trenches and in inadequate billets. Yet where were staff officers supposed to stay? Chateau provided accommodation, offices, telephone communications, lighting and the potential for large scale cooking. They were the ideal places to use as headquarters, and any old fool can be uncomfortable. Presumably the critics would be happier if they sat in a shell hole somewhere? The competence of staff officers can be questioned and perhaps there was excessively luxurious living in a number of cases, but the occupation of a chateau as such does not seem a valid form of criticism. In any case, come the battle, all these higher formations had Advanced HQs, such as Byng's in the ruins of Berthonval farm, or Haig on his train.

From here **head east on the D54** and after three kilometres or so take the **left turn** to Haut Avesnes. Just outside the village is a small British cemetery. Some of the early burials are of members of the 60th (London) Division - this place was used as a rest and recuperation centre by the division for medical cases not considered serious enough to be sent down the line. There are Chinese Labour Corps buried here as well, many from after the war; these may have died as a consequence of an explosives accident whilst clearing the battlefields after the armistice or, more likely, from the virulent epidemic of Spanish 'flu

that swept Europe and beyond after the war and claimed even more lives than that conflict. There are also a few British soldiers buried in the communal cemetery by the main road. This village was also the home of the 60th Divisional train - that is its stores and back up.

*From Acq **take the D62** to Haute-Avesnes - at the main road the communal cemetery of that village is facing you.

Turn **east on the N39** towards Arras and after several kilometres **turn right** on the D60 signposted Anzin, St Aubin and Louez. After half a kilometre or so **turn right** (indicated by a CWGC sign) for Louez cemetery. Take the spur coming off the road just before going under the motorway bridge, which brings you to a Motorway Maintenance area, with the cemetery on your right.

Return to the **main road** and **take the D60E** (ie **turn left** at a crossroads) towards Maroeuil. Head towards the station but before crossing the lines **head right** on a road signposted to Bray. At the edge of Maroeuil there is a CWGC sign for Maroeuil British Cemetery.

Return to the road and **proceed through Bray** which several contemporary accounts described as a delightful spot with swimming in

the river and protection from enemy observation provided from the ridge and the wood on its east. **Continue towards** Ecoivres. The British Cemetery extension at Ecoivres becomes visible on your left, and the entrance is at this the southern edge of the cemetery. At the main road **turn left**, and by the parish church **turn left again** and stop. The large building is a chateau which was used by Currie as his (1st) Divisional Headquarters for the battle. Canon Scott noted,

'My alarm clock went off at four am on the great day of April 9th, which will always shine brightly in the annals of the war. I got up and ate the breakfast which I had prepared the night before, and taking with me my tin of bully beef, I started off to see the opening barrage. It was quite dark when I emerged from the door of the chateau and passed the sentry at the gate. I went through the village of Ecoivres, past the crucifix of the cemetery, and then turning to the right up to Bray Hill on the St Eloi road.'
[*The Great War As I Saw It.*]

He went off and sat on his own away from the other watchers until at 5.30am the barrage began,

'There was so much human suffering and sorrow, there was such tremendous issues involved in that fierce attack, there was such splendour of human character being manifested now in that 'far flung line', where smoke and flame mocked the calm of the morning sky, that the watcher felt he was gazing upon eternal things.'

In the chateau at Ecoivres the count who owned it kept some rooms downstairs for himself.

'In the hall upstairs we had a large model of Vimy Ridge, which all the officers and men of the battalions visited in turn, in order to study the character of the land over which they had to charge. In the garden were numerous huts, and in a large building in a street to the right of the Chateau was a billet which held a great number of men. It was almost entirely filled up with tiers upon tiers of wooden shelves on which the men made their beds. They were reached by wooden stairs. Nearly 1500 men were crowded into the building.'

The village school in Ecoivres was used as a Main Dressing Station.

**Return** the way you came, halting at the car park for the communal cemetery This is Scott's description after the battle was over,

'The aftermath of victory is, of course, very sad. Many were the gallant men whose bodies were laid to rest in the little[!] cemetery at Ecoivres. The cemetery is well kept and very prettily situated. The relatives of those buried here will be pleased to find the graves so carefully preserved. The large crucifix which stands on a mound near the gate is most picturesquely surrounded by trees. In the mound some soldier, probably a Frenchman, had once made a dug-out. The site was evidently chosen with the idea that crucifixes were untouched by shells and therefore places of refuge from danger.'

Follow the road up the hill and through the wood to the D341. If you have time, look at Canon Scott's view.

**Turn right** and at the crossroads at the bottom of the road, should you wish to return to the Arras - Bethune road, **turn left** on the road signposted Cambrai.

# THE CEMETERIES

This section is longer than in my earlier books. In recent years the obnoxious custom of removing registers from cemeteries has increased to epidemic proportions. More detail is now included of information that can also be found in the introduction to a cemetery's entry in a register. It is an easy matter to purchase a copy of a register from the CWGC and for a reasonable fee it is possible to borrow a number for a period of time; there really is no excuse for this anti-social behaviour of stealing books that are an essential part of a pilgrim's visit to the battlefields.

1. Arras Memorial Fauborg d'Amiens Cemetery.
2. Cabaret Rouge British Cemetery.
3. Canadian Cemetery No. 2.
4. Ecoivres Military Cemetery.
5. Givenchy-en-Gohelle Canadian Cemetery.
6. Givenchy Road Canadian Cemetery.
7. La Targette British Cemetery (Aux-Rietz).
8. Lichfield Crater.
9. Louez Military Cemetery.
10. Maroeuil British Cemetery.
11. Nine Elms Military Cemetery.
12. Petit Vimy British Cemetery.
13. Sucrerie Cemetery.
14. Thelus Military Cemetery.
15. Villers Station Cemetery.
16. Zivy Crater.
17. Zouave Valley Cemetery.

## 1. The Arras Memorial and Fauborg d'Amiens Cemetery

This is a most impressive memorial to the 35,698 men who were killed in the area between Loos in the north and Berles au Bois in the south between the spring of 1916 to August 7th 1918, and who have no known grave. The memorial does not include those killed and missing in the Cambrai battle who are separately commemorated on their own memorial. This number does include all

189

those members of the British flying services killed on the whole of the Western Front and who have no known grave. Soldiers of Canada, Australia and Newfoundland (which was not a Province of Canada until after World War II) are commemorated not here but on their various national memorials.

When the policy concerning cemeteries and memorials was being discussed after the war, the French government had decided views on how much land was to be taken up by them. In December 1915 a law was passed giving the land on which British and Commonwealth cemeteries were built in perpetuity as a perpetual resting place. The British policy on cemeteries was not to concentrate them, as did all the other combatants to a greater or lesser degree, but to try and leave as many as possible as they were created during the conflict. For the modern visitor to the battlefields these cemeteries frequently provide the most telling visible sign that a battle or conflict of some sort had taken place when now all around is peaceful farmland or urban bustle.

The French feared that in the post war period hundreds of memorials would be put up all over the old battlefields, not only by governments but also by regimental associations and grieving families. They instituted quite vigorous procedures to prevent great tracts of land being taken up with innumerable memorials, great and small. The decision was taken that only two British memorials solely for the missing would be allowed in France. Any other such memorials would have to be part of an existing plot of land given as a cemetery. The two British memorials in France that qualified under this arrangement were at La Ferte sous Jouarre and Soissons, but they are both small. Therefore the Thiepval Memorial was to be just for the missing, but a stroke of genius created the joint Anglo-French cemetery that is situated on its western side.

The cemetery at Arras was originally opened for French military burials; their military hospital was in a nearby convent. It was also used for civilian burials for a time, as the communal cemetery was on the eastern side of the city and under constant German shell fire. On the arrival of the British in the area in March 1916 it became the burial place for units which served in and around the city and for the Field Ambulances that were based there. After the war ended 207

British graves were concentrated to the cemetery, and at the same time 770 French military graves removed, as well as the civilian burials.

*Whilst here it is worth a visitor's while to continue along the rather undistinguished road by the memorial to the Mur des Fusilees. This is a point in the defences of the Citadel where the Gestapo executed various members of the Resistance during World War II. Even the most bubbly of school parties is affected by this wretched and evil spot.*

## 2. Cabaret Rouge British Cemetery

Cabaret Rouge is to the south of Souchez which was completely destroyed in the war. After the Armistice Souchez was adopted by the Royal Borough of Kensington, with the intention of helping the community to get back on its feet by assisting with rebuilding and resourcing the village. Men from Kensington fought in the area whilst serving with the 56th and 60th London Divisions in the 1/13th and 2/13th (Kensingtons) London Regiment.

The Cabaret Rouge was a house some two hundred yards or so to the east of the road, opposite the cemetery. There was heavy fighting here in the French offensive of May 1915, and this house and the track before it (the Chemin des Pylones) marked the limit of the French advance. The banks opposite the cemetery provided dug-outs for battalion and brigade headquarters, whilst a long communication trench to the rear (Cabaret Road) came out from the present cemetery grounds onto the Arras - Bethune road, and continued on its way to the front line as Ersatz Avenue.

The cemetery was begun in March 1916 by the 47th (London) Division and was used until September 1918. These original burials, about 500 of them, are in Plots I to V, to the right of the cemetery entrance beyond the ring of graves. That these are the original graves is given away to some extent by their unsymmetrical positioning. After the war Cabaret Rouge was turned into a massive concentration cemetery not only for isolated graves in the Arras but for 103 other burial grounds in the Nord and Pas de Calais. Famous spots such as 'Windy Corner' near Richebourg-l'Avoue are represented here by 250 or so soldiers who were buried at the two Edward Road cemeteries at that place. Bodies have come from as far away as Abeele, on the Franco-Belgian border. Many were in German cemeteries, which had to be removed after the war and concentrated, and the remaining British graves were too few to merit their own cemetery. The total number concentrated was 7,191 and the cemetery is the biggest British one in the Arras area and the second largest in France after Étaples.

### 3. Canadian Cemetery No. 2

The cemetery lies within the boundaries of the Canadian Memorial Park and this has on occasion made access by car difficult as the approach road is sometimes chained off.

The cemetery was created after the capture of the ridge and was a burial place for those killed on April 9th and soon thereafter in the battle for Vimy Ridge. It was one of a number of cemeteries established by the Corps Burial Officer, hence its name. It was used as a concentration cemetery for many years after the war for isolated graves and those bodies which were found in the area over the years. There are just under 3,000 buried here of which two thirds are British and the remaining third overwhelmingly Canadian. Over 2,000 are unknown and of the named graves over half are Canadians.

At the south east edge of the cemetery, passing in a roughly west to east direction, was Central Avenue or Boyau Centrale which features prominently in this book.

The concentration nature of the cemetery throws up some interesting anomalies. How did Sjt Harry Boon, 2/KOYLI, who was killed on October 18th 1914 end up here; or CSM James Burfield, 2/Queen's, killed on May 16th 1915 or, even more mysteriously, Cpl Terence Lahee of Queen Victoria's Rifles, killed on July 1st 1916 when his battalion was attacking the Germans at Gommecourt on the Somme? The register sometimes provides more than a bare summary of a man's name, regiment and number and family details.

From the end of the cemetery there are views over the British support lines, and across the motorway (which is concealed by a cutting here) may be seen the portal of the cemetery at Cabaret Rouge.

### 4. Ecoivres Military Cemetery

This cemetery completely dominates the communal cemetery of which it is an extension. The civilian cemetery serves the inhabitants of Ecoivres and Mont St Eloi. The French had buried over 1,000 men before the British took over the line in March 1916. The cemetery became so large because it was easy to bring casualties and the dead from the front on the military tramway. This took out trench supplies and equipment on the outward journey and was the ideal method for bringing the bodies back for decent burial. This in turn explains the rare chronological arrangement of the burials - from the first row to the last the men are buried almost exactly in the order of their death.

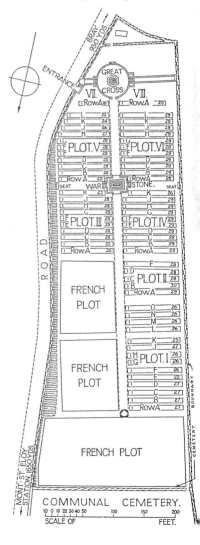

There are 1735 graves in the British part of the cemetery - 891 are British, 828 Canadian, 4 South African and 2 Australian. There are ten Germans who died as prisoners of war.

*'On the further side of the wood, east of Mont St Eloi, lay a large military cemetery, la cimetiere de la Motte, containing many hundreds of French and British graves. Some were surrounded with railings of wood or iron; many had wreaths - one very pretty one was of artificial violets. In several cases the only clue to the man resting there was his name on a slip of paper inside a bottle laid on the grave; but most were marked by large or small wooden crosses. Frequently one saw a shattered rifle with its muzzle stuck in the mound of earth; and on the butt a soldier's bullet-holed kepi or a metal helmet dinted or perforated in a manner tell-tale of how the owner had died.'* (A Medico's Luck in the War.)

Private Fraser noted on February 14th 1917 that, *'the last two to be buried were members of the Canadian Black watch, the 42nd. They were interred yesterday. A few days before an unknown German soldier was buried beside his*

193

*opponents.'* On April 6th his diary entry reads, *'Fritz sent over a solitary shell which crashed into the middle of a hut occupied by a party of Royal Engineers, killing fourteen and wounding eighteen. I happened to be looking at the spot when it struck. It is about three hundred yards away and below Mont St Eloy'* (The Journal of Private Fraser.) These casualties described by Private Fraser may all be found by simply looking along the rows until a proximate date is found; there is a long line of fourteen Royal Engineers who were killed on April 6th.

**5.Givenchy-en-Gohelle Canadian Cemetery** The cemetery was begun in March 1917 and given the name of CD 20 and was used for only two months until May, although a couple of burials were added in March 1918. It is, therefore, a battlefield cemetery - that is it contains burials of men who were killed or died near the spot and was not used as a place to bring scattered burials after the war ended. It lies a hundred and fifty yards or so due east from the site of Ersatz Crater and is about two hundred yards south east of the Gunner/Montreal group of craters. There was a Canadian cemetery near Gunner's Crater, but their graves were lost. There are 154 buried in this cemetery, of whom 144 are known to be Canadian. The rough track running eastwards beside the cemetery is not suitable for most vehicles; the Crosbie craters are a few hundred yards along this and to the right in the (private) woodland.

The earliest burial is that of Rifleman Alfred Bray of the London Irish Rifles who died in May 1916. Of those who are identified, the vast majority are casualties of the attack on Vimy Ridge, most on April 9th.

## 6. Givenchy Road Cemetery

This cemetery was established after the battle for Vimy Ridge and all but half a dozen of the 111 buried here were killed in the fighting on April 9th. Apart from a couple of casualties from the PPCLI and the Machine Gun Company all were

members of either the 1st or 2nd Central Ontario Regiment (54th, 75th and 102nd Battalions). It is close to Canadian Cemetery No. 2 (this one was originally CD 1) and shares the same access road within the Canadian Memorial Park.

### 7. La Targette British Cemetery (Aux Rietz)

The cemetery is dwarfed by its French neighbour, a concentration cemetery which also contains, in the part closest to the British cemetery, a large number of casualties, including some Belgians, from fighting in the area during 1940. The British cemetery was started at the end of April 1917 when the cemetery was safely in the rear area; before that date the cross roads was a favourite target of the German artillery. Although there was a Field Ambulance post close to the cross roads from March 1916 the dead were removed by tramway to the cemetery at Maroeuil or Ecoivres. The cemetery was in use until September 1918, at which time the war had moved on from the area. This was a battlefield cemetery and only sixteen graves were concentrated here after the war out of a total of 679, of which forty one are unknown. Almost a third of those buried here belonged to artillery units. Indeed, in the battle for Vimy Ridge the artillery headquarters of the 2nd (Canadian) and 5th (Imperial) Divisions, as well as some Heavy Artillery units were in the caves on the east side of the Arras road. Many other burials belonged to support arms - Labour Companies, Railway Troops, Ammunition Columns, Canadian Infantry Works Battalions, Field Survey Companies and Army Service Corps.

There are several who are buried here who invite comment. Major Samuel Doake DSO of the Royal Field Artillery was killed on March 30th 1918, but his DSO was not gazetted until June 3rd 1918, as part of the King's Birthday Honours list. He passed second into the Royal Military Academy Woolwich and was commissioned into the Royal Artillery in 1912. He landed in France in August 1914 and served continuously at the front thereafter. 2/Lt P Innes was

killed in action on April 30th 1917 at the age of 19; a year earlier he had been the Head of School at Haileybury and was waiting to proceed to Trinity, Cambridge as a History Scholar. Perhaps the most significant burial is that of Lt Col AEE Lowry DSO MC, commanding officer of 2/West Yorks. He was killed by a machine gun bullet on September 23rd 1918 whilst out visiting his battalion's outpost line when it was serving in the Willerval sector. He was born in 1892 and was educated at Cheltenham and Sandhurst, where he was a Prize Cadet and won the French Prize. He was commissioned into the West Yorks in 1913 and became Adjutant in March 1915. He commanded the battalion for over a year and was only 24 when appointed. He won his DSO for his actions during the Battle of the Aisne in May/June 1918, when his battalion was working with 2/Dorsets as part of 23 Brigade, 8th Division. 2/Dorsets were to gain immortal fame for their action in the Bois des Buttes. Lowry's citation reads, 'For conspicuous gallantry and devotion to duty during many days of very fierce fighting, when he led counter-attacks against overwhelming odds, and restored situations after the enemy had broken through; and finally, when surrounded on all sides, he cut his way out, being personally the last to cover the withdrawal. He

was overpowered and captured, but during the night escaped from his escort, and made his way back across many miles at the greatest personal risk. His fortitude and indomitable courage throughout a memorable twelve days were beyond all praise.'

### 8. Lichfield Crater

This unusual cemetery (along with its near neighbour, Zivy Crater) was used by the Canadian Corps Burial Officer as a burial place after the fighting of April 1917. It is that unusual thing amongst British cemeteries, a mass grave. A total of 58 are buried there, including an unknown

Russian soldier (how did he get there?) and all are probably Canadian with the exception of Pte Albert Stubbs of 8/South Lancs. He was killed on April 30th 1916 whilst his battalion was serving with the 25th Division and was found on the edge of the crater when the battlefield was being cleared of bodies and isolated graves after the armistice.

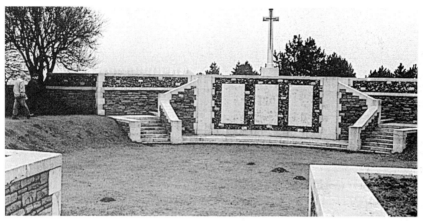

The names of the dead are carved on panels under the Cross of Sacrifice. Amongst these is the name of L/Sgt Ellis Welwood Sifton of the 18th Bn (Western Ontario Regt) CEF who won the Victoria Cross on April 9th.

*'For most conspicuous bravery and devotion to duty. During the attack in enemy trenches Sergeant Sifton's Company was held by machine-gun fire which inflicted many casualties. Having located the gun he charged it single-handed, killing all the crew. A small enemy party advanced down the trench, but he succeeded in keeping these off until our men had gained the position. In carrying out this gallant act he was killed, but his conspicuous valour undoubtedly saved many lives and contributed largely to the success of the operation.'*

This puts his actions simply. He had held off the advancing enemy with his bayonet and eventually used the rifle as a club. The fighting had stopped when more Canadians came up but a wounded German shot Sifton as he was marshalling the prisoners.

### 9. Louez Military Cemetery

This is a difficult cemetery for the uninitiated to find. Although it is well signposted off the D60 at Louez there are no other signs. The situation has been complicated by the recent construction of a part of the Arras ring road which runs just behind the cemetery. The cemetery is near a spur running off the track just before it goes under the new road - it is a highway maintenance area, so do not be put off by No Entry Signs.

As for many of the cemeteries in the area, this one was originally commenced by the French and the British took it over on their arrival on this front. The French graves, as is also usual, have been removed, in this case to Notre Dame de

Lorette. The cemetery was used by the 51st (Highland) Division and then by their replacements in the Roclincourt/Ecurie sector, the 60th (London) Division. In turn the Canadian Mounted Rifles used it from November 1916 to March 1917. There are 204 British and Canadian burials. The register incorrectly states that the two Germans buried here have been removed.

The Regimental History of 1/4th Seaforth Highlanders explains the presence of one of these Germans:

*'About seven am [on June 3rd] a German deserter tried to get over in broad daylight. He crawled for the British Line with a little white flag in his hand; then, when halfway over, sprang up and ran for it, but was shot down by his own side. After dark Lt Mills and L/Cpl Bessent went over and found him dead. He was so heavy that two stretcher bearers had to be fetched to bring him to Headquarters. He proved to be a Lorrainer. It was evident that for some time he had meant to desert, but no documents of value were found on him.'*

### 10. Maroeuil British Cemetery

This cemetery was begun by the 51st (Highland) Division in March 1916 and almost half of those buried here are from units of that division. Another quarter or so of the burials are those from the 60th (London) Division. As far as possible the bodies were brought back on the tramway that used to run up to the line (the same tramway that passed the Aux Rietz dressing station), and this has meant that the bodies are, by and large, buried in chronological order of their death. The cemetery is protected from observation by the hill to its east. It is beside a track that is in a very poor state of repair and is a cemetery that seems to be rarely visited.

### 11. Nine Elms Military Cemetery

This was the cemetery that was started by the 13th Bn CEF on the eve of April 9th; these original burials are to be found in Plot I Row A. They were packed so closely together that one headstone has to make do, in a number of cases, for two or three casualties. Rows A and B were filled by June 1917 and only three more burials (in Row C) were made, in July 1918, before the end of the war. After the Armistice 499 British and 231 French graves were concentrated to the cemetery, although subsequently 177 French graves were removed to other cemeteries, leaving 54 behind. There is no obvious explanation for this strange decision. The French dead are almost entirely from the fighting of 1914 and 1915. The British concentrations came from nearby cemeteries, the furthest afield being the 58 who were buried just to the south of Hill 145.

The cultural diversity of Canada is shown by the grave of Pte Iwakichi Kojima who was killed aged 38 on April 9th whilst serving with the 10th Bn CEF; his parents living still in Tochigiken in Japan.

The cemetery is situated in a slight hollow and so does not boast extensive views of the battlefield to the west - it does show how a slight rise can make a considerable difference in such a generally featureless landscape.

### 12. Petit Vimy Cemetery

This is a small cemetery on the eastern side of Vimy Ridge. It is best to reach it by parking at la Justice and walking through the woods down to the cemetery - this is a walk of only some ten minutes. The signposted access is by a very poor track from Petit Vimy - and it is quite difficult enough to get into this hamlet! It was a cemetery used in the months following the capture of Vimy Ridge, and by the end of the war there were 63 men buried there. 27 were concentrated to the cemetery after the war. One of these was 2/Lt Eric Welch of 16th Squadron RFC who was killed in aerial combat on April 23rd 1917 - one of the many RFC victims during what the Flying Corps called 'Bloody April'.

### 13. Sucrerie Cemetery

This cemetery can easily be missed if a sharp eye is not kept out for it. It is situated on the eastern edge of Ablain St Nazaire, on the road to Souchez. The sign for the cemetery is on the south side of the road and if coming from Ablain this is completely obscured by a tree. The cemetery is quite visible on the rising ground to the south if coming from Souchez, but in the opposite direction it is hidden by buildings.

The cemetery is now named after the famous sugar factory around which such heavy fighting took place in May and June 1915. This has gone and been replaced by a large farm. The cemetery was commenced, alongside a large French one, in April 1917, presumably because it was safe to use once the German observation from the Pimple had been removed. The large French cemetery, with its 1900 burials, was removed after the war (presumably to Notre Dame de Lorette).

It was originally called Saskatchewan Cemetery, possibly because it was started by men from the 46th (South Saskatchewan) Bn of the CEF. It provides good views of the Lorette spur, Ablain and the road to Souchez - a good spot from which to view some of the heavy fighting described in the first chapter.

## 14. Thelus Military Cemetery

This is an extremely isolated cemetery, but yet clearly visible for some distance. It stands about 300 yards on the west side of the Lens - Arras road, just before Thelus if heading south. The visitor is faced with no obvious parking place for the car off a very busy road and there is a considerable walk down a long but narrow lawn strip across open fields. The visitors' book indicates about ten visits a year, though obviously maybe three or four times that number actually come to the cemetery. Road developments in recent years have detracted from the excellent views it had to the east, though these are still extensive.

## 15. Villers Station Cemetery

The cemetery is next to the railway line that used to run between Frevent and Lens which was largely used for conveying sugar beet and other farm products. The line ran eastwards from here through Carency and then to Souchez and beyond. Once more, the railway line was a convenient way of bringing the dead to a secure place for burial. The British started using this cemetery, already established by the French, in July 1916. The 2,000 or so French graves were removed in June 1923 for the most part to Notre Dame de Lorette. The crucifix that used to be at Carency Church was kept in a shed by the roadside here, and after the war it was restored to that church.

Close to the cemetery but well hidden behind trees is the Chateau de la Haie which was frequently in use as a divisional or corps Headquarters. The old station house still exists and seems to be inhabited, although I have never seen the shutters open. With great care it is possible to drive down the old railway track to Carency.

## 16. Zivy Crater Cemetery

The cemetery is a mass burial in Zivy Crater. There are 53 buried here, almost certainly all Canadian as those who are known (48 of them) are all from that army and were all killed on April 9th 1917. Perhaps unintentionally, it is a moving combination of memorial to the tunnellers, marker of the old front line occupied for so many months before April 1917 and memorial to the men of Canada who were able to push the enemy off their formidable position.

Views from the cemetery are severely limited, especially to the east, as the Calais - Paris motorway stands squarely in the way. Looking westwards there are views to Neuville St Vaast and along the site of the line of the craters that ran southwards, the positions held by Germans and, for example, the men of the 60th (London) Division. The road that runs by the cemetery is the old one that ran to Thelus from Neuville St Vaast.

## 17. Zouave Valley Cemetery

The cemetery is in an isolated spot south of Souchez; the valley is named after the Zouaves, light infantrymen recruited from Algeria who wore a most distinctive uniform, who fought here so bravely in 1914 - 1915. The cemetery is very close to the site of Wortley Avenue (originally Boyau 1,2,3), a communication trench coming from the west, and International Avenue, Gordon Avenue and Vincent Street just beyond to the east. The motorway is at the top of the steep embankment to the east, the Talus des Zouaves. The cemetery was commenced in May 1916 and was in use until June 1917. After the Armistice 42 isolated graves from an area around Souchez were concentrated here. They are all in Plot I, in neat rows. The battlefield nature of the rest of the cemetery is indicated by the rather more haphazard arrangement.

Some of the earliest burials are members of the Royal Fusiliers, who were killed in the aftermath of the German attack on the 47th (London) Division on May 21st. These included the 22nd (Kensingtons) and 23rd and 24th (1st and 2nd Sportsmen's) Battalions which were members of 99 Brigade, 2nd Division. The cemetery would seem to have been begun by those units which were not customarily in the line here - prior to this the dead were usually removed by tramway - and it could also be that this means of taking away the dead was temporarily halted by the force of the German bombardment. Whatever the reason, the cemetery was not particularly well sited if eternal earthly rest was an objective, as the cemetery suffered considerably from shell fire.

The road to the west leads to the Chemin des Pylones, which is passable towards Souchez but not advised towards Neuville. The track to the south by the cemetery is usually passable, however, even if it does not look too promising, and will bring you into Neuville.

# The Memorials

1. French Memorial in Givenchy Wood (Bois de l'Abime).
2. 44th Battalion CEF Memorial, The Pimple.
3. The Vimy Memorial to the Missing.
4. Moroccan Division Memorial.
5. 3rd (Canadian) Divison Memorial, La Folie Farm.
6. Polish Memorial and Czech Memorial and Cemetery.
7. Isolated tombs near Neuville St Vaast.
8. Canadian Artillery Memorial, Thelus.
9. La Targette Memorial.
10. War Memorial, Communal Cemetery Neuville St Vaast.
11. Aspirant Augustin Leuregans Memorial.

### 1. French Memorial in Givenchy Wood

Deep in the wood to the east of Givenchy is an isolated tomb-like memorial to two French soldiers who were killed on the 9th May 1915 in the attack on the Pimple. They were Louis Pique and Maurice Cabrielle of the 'G' Class 1914 - 1915 and were members of the 413th Infantry Regiment. Access to the wood is difficult and one must always take extreme care when the hunting season is on. The memorial is by a track that enters the wood from the north east side of Givenchy. The wood itself shows plentiful signs of heavy fighting and entrenched positions.

### 2. 44th Battalion CEF Memorial, The Pimple

This is the remnant of a memorial that was erected by the battalion in February 1918. The memorial was designed and built by members of the battalion whilst the special cement on which were written the names of the men killed or missing was taken from within the German lines. For various reasons the belief took root that because of the building of the huge Canadian Memorial at Vimy on Hill 145 that the 44th Battalion memorial would have to be demolished. This is a strange reason as the memorials are almost a mile apart. Whatever, the decision was taken to remove the panels to St James Park in Winnipeg where they were rededicated and became the focus of the 44th Battalion's remembrance gatherings on Decoration Day in the spring. What has been left is the concrete shell that contained the panels, surmounted with the legend '44' and 'Canada' at the top of each side.

The memorial was erected on the edge of Irish Crater, itself the southernmost of a group which included New Cut, Mildren, Broadbridge and Football. Mine craters were blown into other mine craters, thus making it practically impossible to move in this area without slipping down steep slopes or having to clamber across ground that had been severely disturbed. The Pimple itself is a few yards inside Givenchy Wood, about a hundred yards down the track towards Souchez, coming down the north side of the ridge. The craters have all gone, filled in with the spoil from the autoroute cutting, which has also served to distort the ground by raising the level of the fields around about.

Access to the memorial is difficult. There are two alternatives. Take the road to Givenchy from the Canadian Memorial; on entering the village there is a sharp left turn (Rue de Gallieni) which is marked as a cul de sac. The road rapidly becomes very poor quality but it is usually passable. Stop at a crossroads where a track falls away towards Givenchy and a wood commences on the right. The 44th Battalion memorial is in a meadow a hundred yards or so from the crossroads. Access seems to be no problem, although this is private land. Another approach is from Souchez. Follow the signs to Givenchy-en-Gohelle Canadian Cemetery but turn left as soon as you go under the motorway. Follow the road until it comes to a dead end. The memorial is clearly visible in the field on your right, and it is easy to walk over a vehicle block to examine the memorial more closely.

### 3. The Vimy Memorial to the Missing

Like it or hate it this is a vast and striking tribute by the people of Canada to their dead of the Great War, and in particular to their missing. There are some (and I am amongst them) who find the memorial at Vancouver Corner in the Ypres Salient, a soldier with arms reversed, a more moving and less complex tribute.

The monument was placed on Hill 145 and from its platform the Plain of Douai stretches before the onlooker, with the view only limited by the weather conditions and the horizon. The memorial appears now at its most impressive from the motorway, that is from the west side; with the passage of years the woods have grown and done much to obscure the memorial from the east. It was designed by Walter Allward and incorporates the memorial to the missing dead of Canada who fell in France - 11,285 of them. Those who were missing in Flanders, 7,024, are commemorated on the Menin Gate. Canada lost a total of 59,544 to all causes in the course of the war, thus the missing account for over 30% of this total.

The two great pylons, towering 120 feet above the base, symbolise the English and French speaking parts of Canada as well as the British and French armies who fought on the ridge. The wall at the front is fifty yards wide by eight high, whilst the memorial is ninety yards wide overall. The memorial is decorated by twenty allegorical carvings. The six figures on the pylons are Charity, Faith, Honour, Justice and Sacrifice. Between the pylons is a dying soldier who is passing on the torch to a comrade. Two reclining figures on the west side represent the mourning parents of Canada. The most impressive figure is that of mourning Canada, facing east towards the enemy and looking down on the tomb below.

The stone for the memorial had to be able to withstand the elements for many years. The retired Roman Emperor Diocletian's palace at Spalato (Split) in Dalmatia had survived the years extremely well (apart from being used as a quarry by the locals) and so this was the stone that was settled upon for the memorial. The stones were sent from Dalmatia and came to Vimy via Venice. These stones were then put in position and over the next ten years were carved in situ by Italian sculptors, the work continuing even over the winter months. There is a large crypt under the monument and one of the pylons is hollow with a steel ladder going up it - the view must be spectacular. The memorial was formally opened in 1936 by one of the few public engagements of Edward VIII as King; this was achieved by removing the Union Jack which covered the figure of Canada Mourning Her Dead.

There is a car park close to the memorial, with a relief map showing dispositions for the attack on April 9th. There is a small information booth here which, like the preserved trenches, is staffed by bi-lingual Canadian students from mid-April to mid-November. The memorial stands in a 250 acre park, given to Canada by the people of France, and adjacent is Vimy Forest.

### 4. The Moroccan Division Memorial

This memorial stands on the left hand side of the Neuville - Givenchy road at the turning point for the Vimy Memorial. It commemorates the achievement of the Moroccans in gaining Hill 140 (the same place, actually, as Hill 145) on May 9th. Additional inscriptions on the rear make references to various nationalities that served in the Foreign Legion components of the division. Nearby may be found reinforced cupolas and other shelters for snipers, machine gunners and observers.

### 5. 3rd (Canadian) Division Memorial, La Folie Farm

This memorial is hidden away in the wood on the road out to the Arras - Lens highway. There is a rather nondescript, and certainly not prominent, sign indicating the memorial's presence over a small gate that leads into the wood. There is no obvious parking available, and the driver has to make the best of whatever space he can find nearby. There is a walk of about a hundred yards through quite thick woodland, and the memorial, in the form of a cross, stands in its own ground. In the winter when the undergrowth has

died down the shell ravaged ground, complete with trench lines is quite clear. Indicated walks through the woods are well worthwhile as the battle scarred surface of the forest floor is quite apparent.

## 6. Polish Memorial and Czech Memorial and Cemetery

These are situated on a high point either side of the Bethune - Arras road to the north of La Targette. They commemorate the sacrifice made by Czech and Polish citizens who fought in the Foreign Legion in this area in 1915. The Czech memorial was extended to become a cemetery; none of those who were killed in 1915 are buried here; most of the casualties are from the Second World War, a number of them airmen.

## 7. Isolated tombs near Neuville St Vaast

There are two of these tomb memorials to the north east of Neuville St Vaast, one on each side of the motorway. Both are difficult to reach. The one on the west side has access via a small slip road off the Neuville - Givenchy road before the motorway bridge. The other is even more difficult and is in the middle of a field that usually has crops growing in it. To reach this follow the road to Lichfield Crater but find a parking place as soon as is practicable after crossing the motorway. The tomb is in the field on your left. In both cases the (French) bodies have been removed, but the markers remain as a memorial.

## 8. Canadian Artillery Memorial, Thelus

This is situated at the crossroads in Thelus, on the north east side. It also commemorates the South African Heavy Artillery. The monument stands above a dug-out, the entrance to which was under the stairs leading up to the memorial. It was unveiled by General Byng on April 9th 1918 at a time when he might be thought to have better things to do, as the Germans had launched the next phase of their massive Spring Offensive against his front on April 5th. However see comments in Tour 5 for a different date and version of events. The memorial is now surrounded by a number of different types of shell of heavy calibre.

## 9. La Targette Memorial

This rather gruesome memorial is on the west side of the cross roads of the D49 with the Arras road. It commemorates the destruction of the village by mining operations which were part of the attack of May 9th 1915.

## 10. War Memorial Communal Cemetery Neuville St Vaast

The cemetery witnessed very heavy fighting at the time of the French 1915 offensives. The war memorial is unusual in that due honour is paid to the various liberating armies, including the British led by General Horne, and the Canadians under their Corps Commander, General Bing (sic).

## 11. Aspirant Augustin Leuregans Memorial

This memorial, with its distinctive clump of trees, is visble from many parts of the battlefield south of Neuville St Vaast and serves as a useful marker. It stands on ground that formed part of Fort Redoubt, whilst battalion headquarters of various units in the line could be found in dug outs carved out of the embankments of the sunken road just to the south of it.

The sentiments expressed on the memorial are ones that we in a more cynical age would find hard to cope with. *'Augustin Leuregans, an officer cadet of the 236th Infantry Regiment, fell here gloriously in his nineteenth year whilst calling out to his Territorials, 'Come on my old dads, you are not going to let your child die on his own.'* I imagine that we all have our own answer to that one. Yet the memorial does indicate an attitude of mind and of determination amongst the French Army of 1915.

204

# FURTHER READING

There is a tremendous amount of literature about Vimy Ridge, rather less about the Battle of Arras. Much of the writing about Vimy is Canadian and can often be rather unbalanced; however, so long as that is born in mind, the books are readable and give a flavour of the occasion as well as setting out the course of events.

**The Canadian Expeditionary Force** Col GWL NIcholson CD. The Queen's Printer, Ottawa. 1962. This is a first rate one volume history of the contribution of a nation and is an outstanding piece of writing of military history. Unfortunately it is a rare book and many UK public libraries turfed them out of their reserve stock some years back.

**Cheerful Sacrifice. The Battle of Arras 1917** J Nicholls. Leo Cooper, Pen and Sword. 1993. This is the most recent history of the Battle (possibly the only one?) and is highly readable.

**The Shadow of Vimy Ridge** K Macksey. William Kimber. 1965. An unusual approach, he looks at Vimy in its wider importance with sections on Marlborough, April 1917 and 1940.

**Vimy Ridge** A McKee. Souvenir Press. 1966. The first full scale history of the battle.

**Vimy!** HF Wood. Macdonald & Co. 1967. As may be seen, one of a rash of books that came out at the time of the fiftieth anniversary of the battle. This one ties in the political consequences of the battle with the military narrative.

**Canada at Vimy** DE Macintyre. Peter Martin Associates. 1967. An account from one who was there and then was a key organiser for the massive Pilgrimage for the unveiling of the memorial in 1936.
**Vimy** P Berton. McClelland and Stewart. 1986. A very popular (and readable) account. On the other hand there are a number of inaccuracies and simplifications and he appears to let national pride run away with him on occasion.

**The Journal of Private Fraser** ed. RH Roy. Sono Nis Press. 1985. One of the outstanding journal accounts of a soldier to be published in recent years. Fraser served throughout the war until severely wounded at Paschendaele.

**Gunner Ferguson's Diary** ed PG Rogers. Lancelot Press 1985. An interesting diary, not least because the writer was clearly quite a difficult character with a very definite mind of his own when it came to authority.

**Byng of Vimy** J Williams. Leo Cooper, Pen and Sword. 1992 (Reprint). A first rate book about this formidable man and an enjoyable read.

**Tunnellers** WG Grieve and B Newman. Reprint, Naval and Military Press. 1995. An excellent and detailed account of the work of tunnellers during the war.

**The War Underground** A Barrie. Frederick Muller Ltd. 1962. A rather more anecdotal history of the work of the tunnellers.

**The Illustrated Michelin Guides to the Battlefields. Arras** c.1921. See end of Chapter 1 for details.

**Before Endeavours Fade** REB Coombs MBE. After the Battle. 1994, completely updated. This book is now on its Seventh Edition, and justly so. It is a tremendous piece of work which has been a vade mecum with battlefield tourers for twenty years now.

# SELECTIVE INDEX